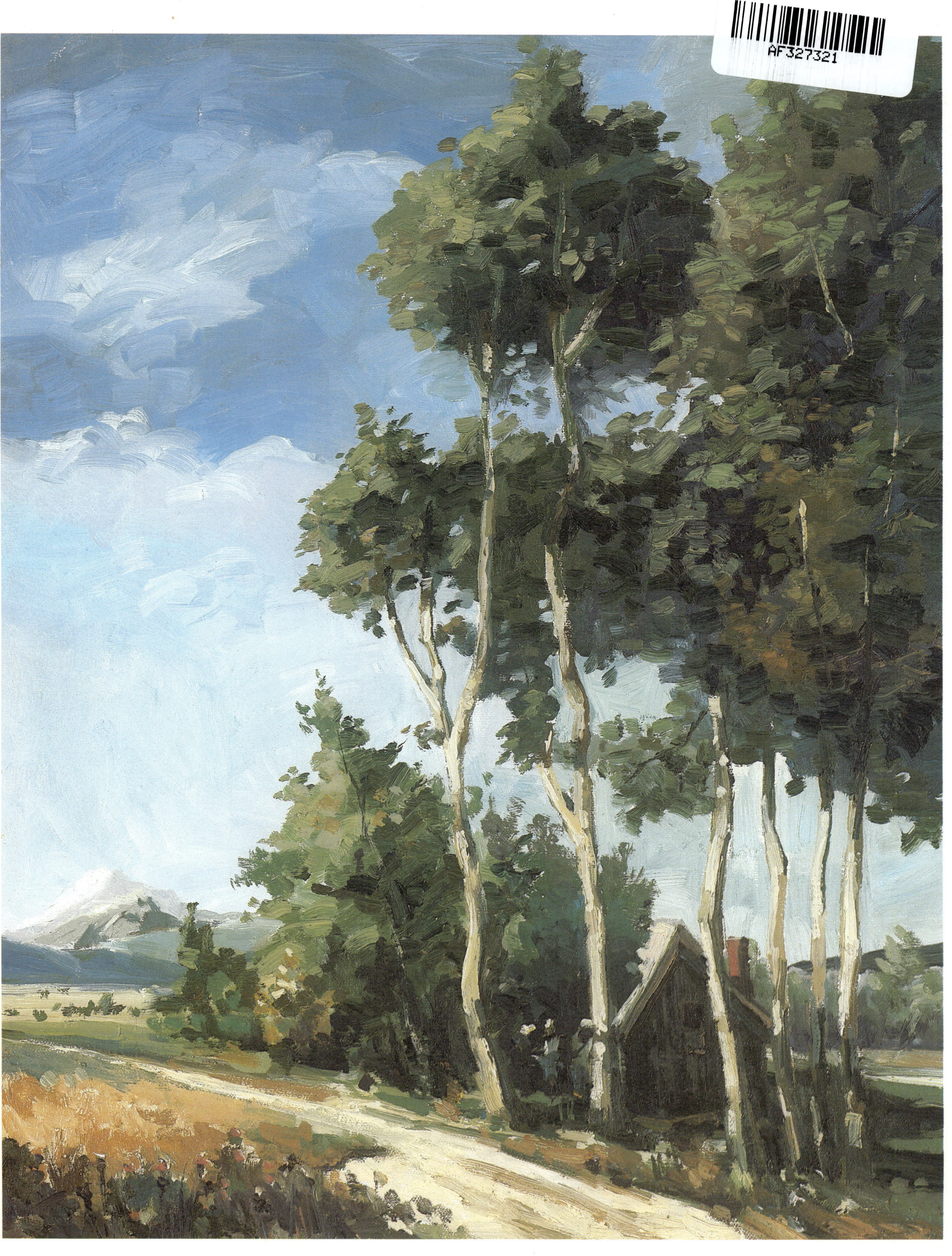
AF327321

TOOLS OF THE TRADE

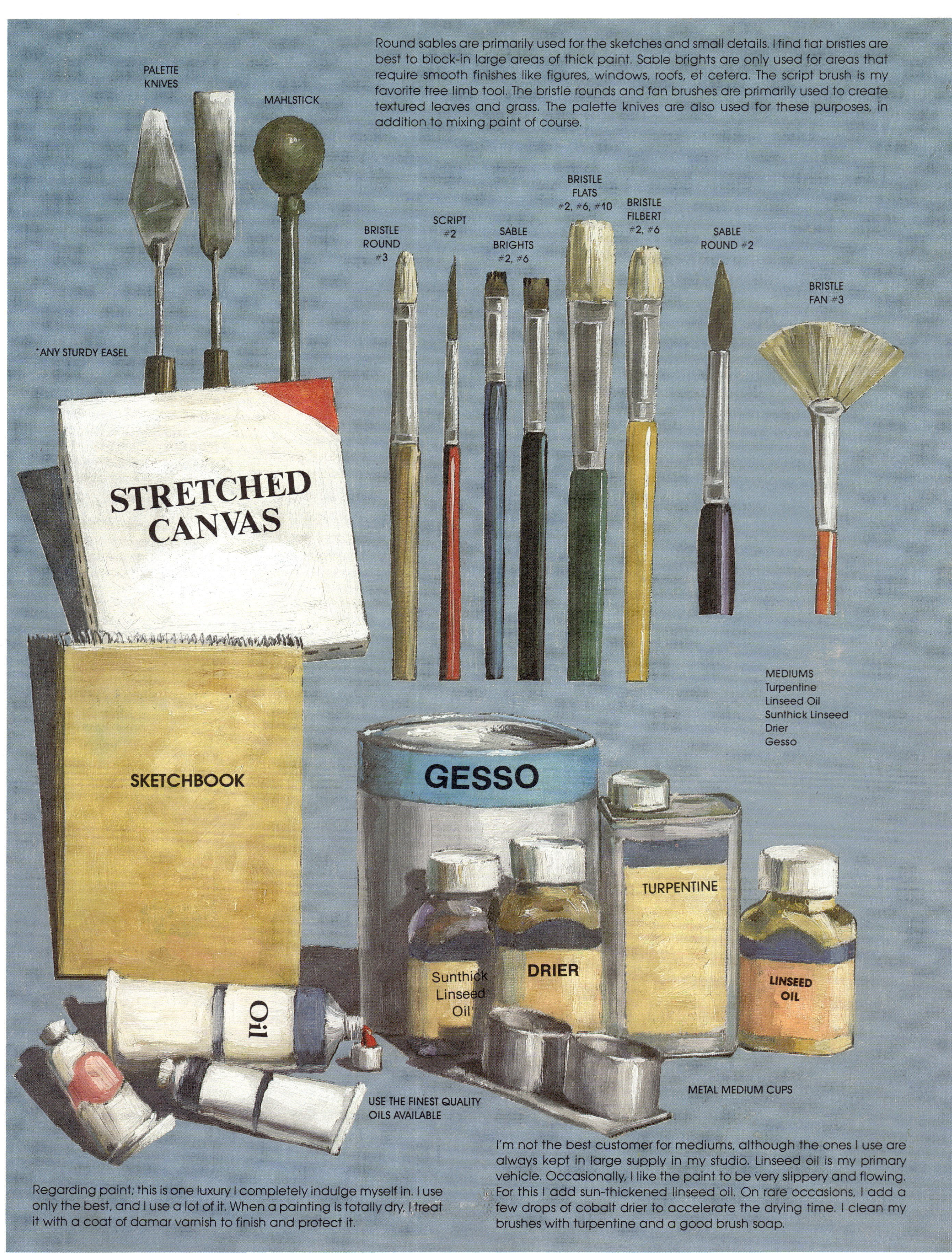

Round sables are primarily used for the sketches and small details. I find flat bristles are best to block-in large areas of thick paint. Sable brights are only used for areas that require smooth finishes like figures, windows, roofs, et cetera. The script brush is my favorite tree limb tool. The bristle rounds and fan brushes are primarily used to create textured leaves and grass. The palette knives are also used for these purposes, in addition to mixing paint of course.

Regarding paint; this is one luxury I completely indulge myself in. I use only the best, and I use a lot of it. When a painting is totally dry, I treat it with a coat of damar varnish to finish and protect it.

I'm not the best customer for mediums, although the ones I use are always kept in large supply in my studio. Linseed oil is my primary vehicle. Occasionally, I like the paint to be very slippery and flowing. For this I add sun-thickened linseed oil. On rare occasions, I add a few drops of cobalt drier to accelerate the drying time. I clean my brushes with turpentine and a good brush soap.

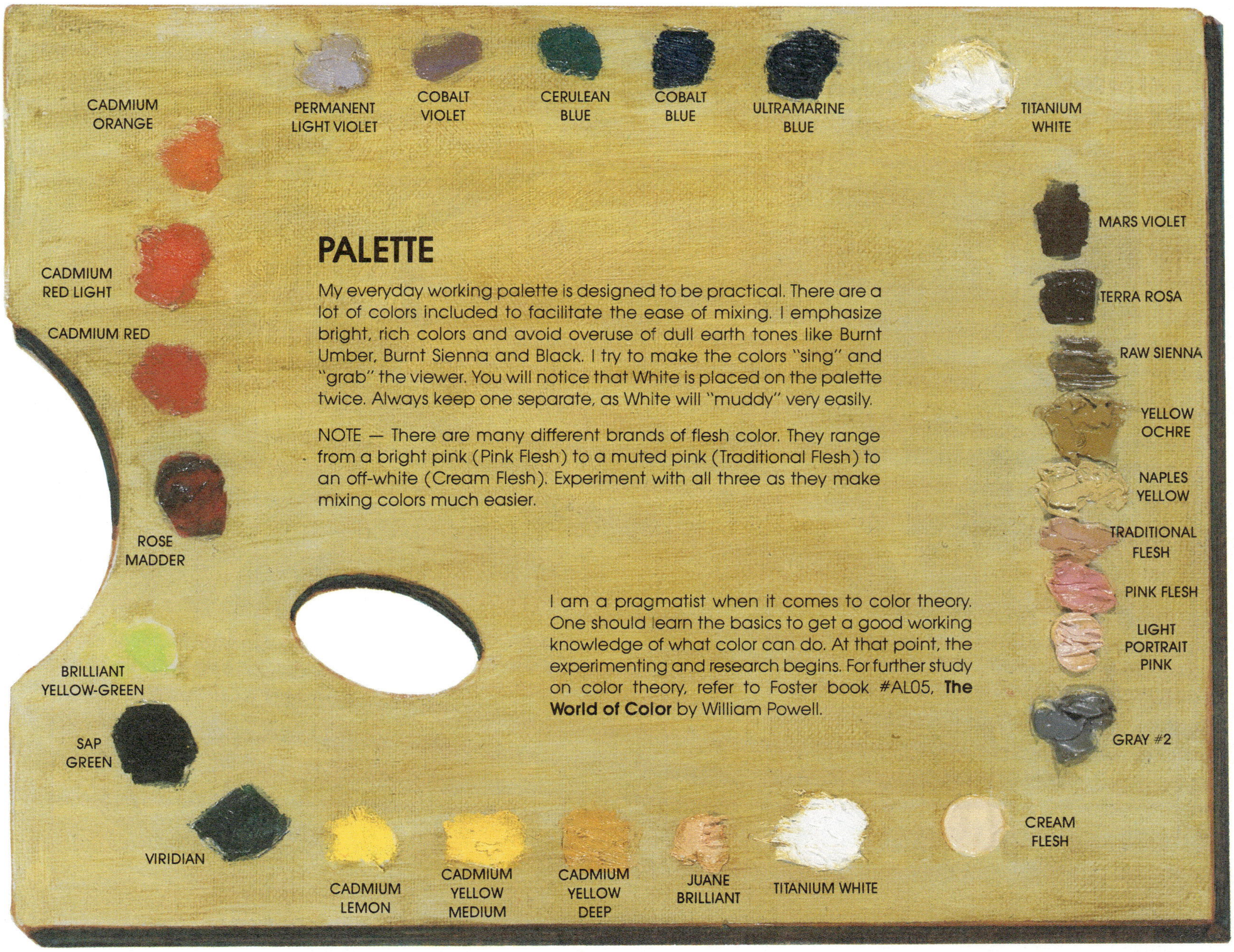

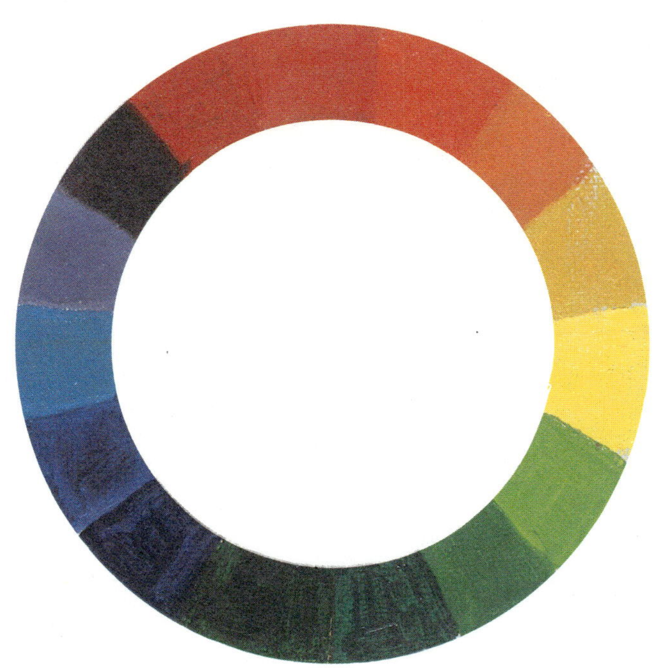

PALETTE

My everyday working palette is designed to be practical. There are a lot of colors included to facilitate the ease of mixing. I emphasize bright, rich colors and avoid overuse of dull earth tones like Burnt Umber, Burnt Sienna and Black. I try to make the colors "sing" and "grab" the viewer. You will notice that White is placed on the palette twice. Always keep one separate, as White will "muddy" very easily.

NOTE — There are many different brands of flesh color. They range from a bright pink (Pink Flesh) to a muted pink (Traditional Flesh) to an off-white (Cream Flesh). Experiment with all three as they make mixing colors much easier.

I am a pragmatist when it comes to color theory. One should learn the basics to get a good working knowledge of what color can do. At that point, the experimenting and research begins. For further study on color theory, refer to Foster book #AL05, **The World of Color** by William Powell.

COLOR WHEEL

The color wheel is a most helpful tool. Among other things, it shows you which colors are complementary to each other. Impressionists use color complements often; for instance, when painting a Yellow object, they use Violet to paint the shadow areas. Likewise, Red to Green and Orange to Blue. You can make different shades of gray by mixing complementary colors plus White, or by mixing all three primary colors.

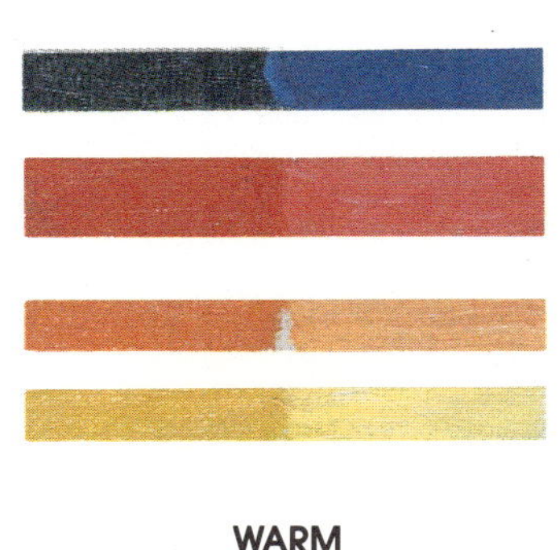
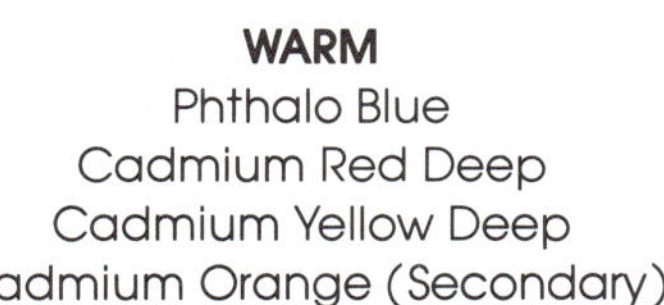

The properties of color that are most important to me are:

1. Value — the darkness or lightness of a color.
2. Warm/Cool color relationships.

Manufactured oil color is not pure, in fact, most colors contain some of all three primaries (red, blue, yellow). Certain colors have a warm tone or cool tone. The purist may wish to have an overall warm or cool tone to a painting. If so, one could mix all ones colors from either of these primary groups:

WARM
Phthalo Blue
Cadmium Red Deep
Cadmium Yellow Deep
Cadmium Orange (Secondary)

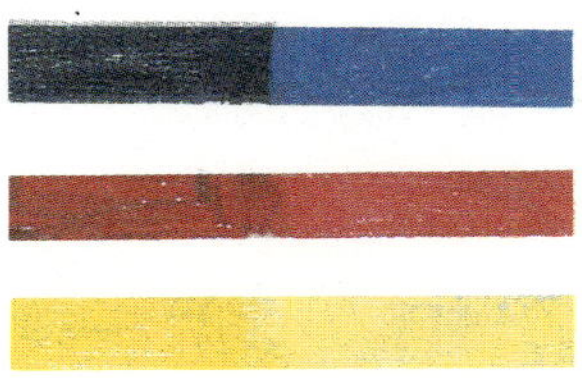

COOL
Ultramarine Blue
Rose Madder
Cadmium Yellow Lemon

The most exciting part of drawing and painting for me is creating the illusion of a three-dimensional object on a two-dimensional surface. If one pays attention to relative lightness or darkness (value) of shapes, this is easily obtained. When painting an old red barn, note the shades of red necessary to depict it.

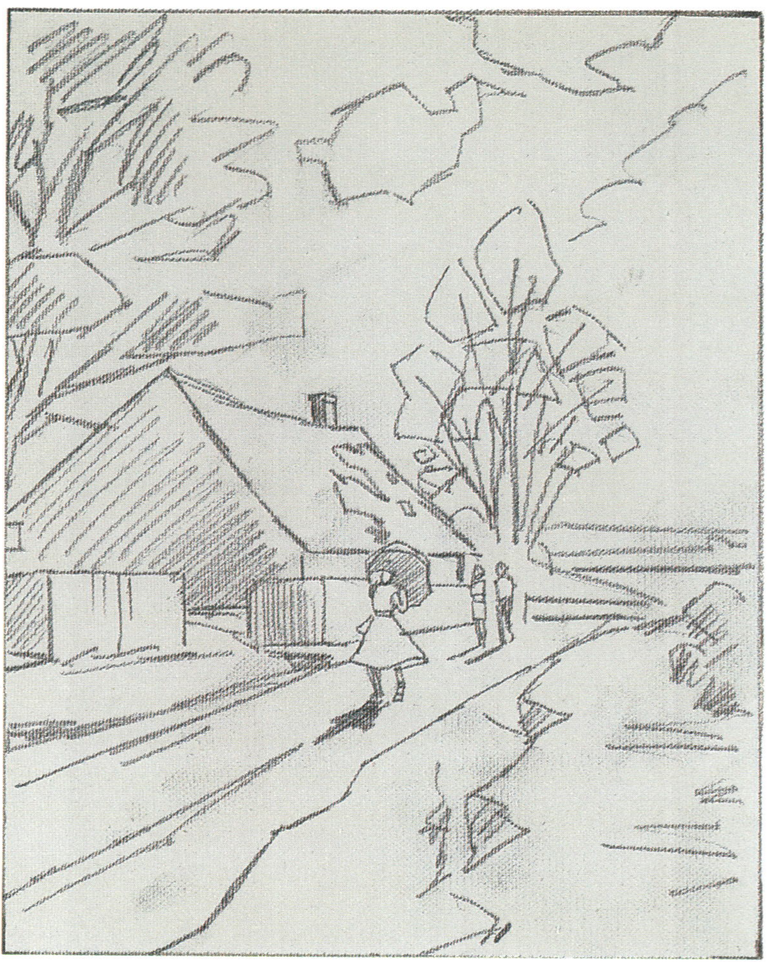

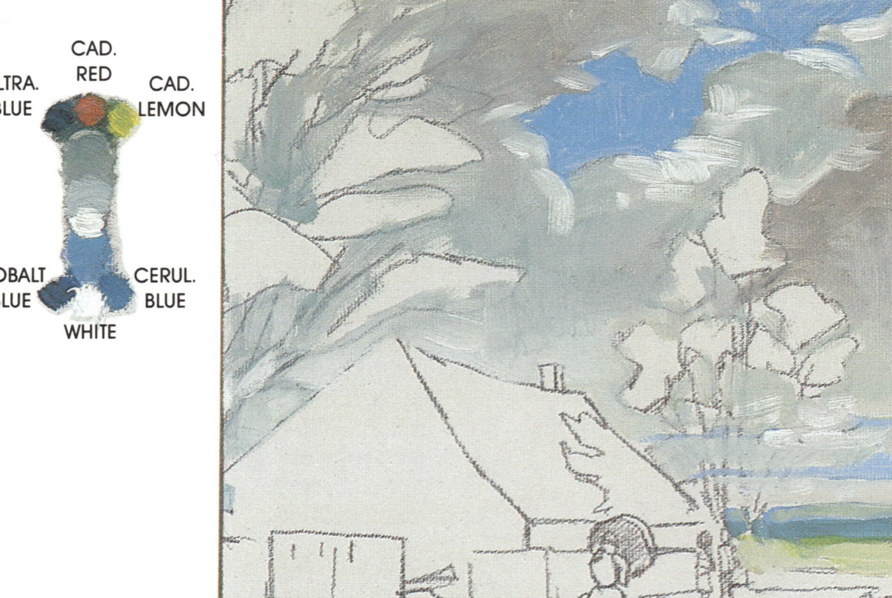

You will notice that all the shapes are reduced to simple squares, triangles, rectangles, and their variations. I do not draw in any real detail, but am very thorough in the initial layout stage. If the figure gives you trouble, do a detailed drawing to refer to.

It is obvious that one must paint the background first. I block-in the dark colors by mixing the primary colors to make various shades of gray. The blue sky peeking through the clouds is a mixture of Cobalt, Cerulean and White. I use only flat bristle brushes for this.

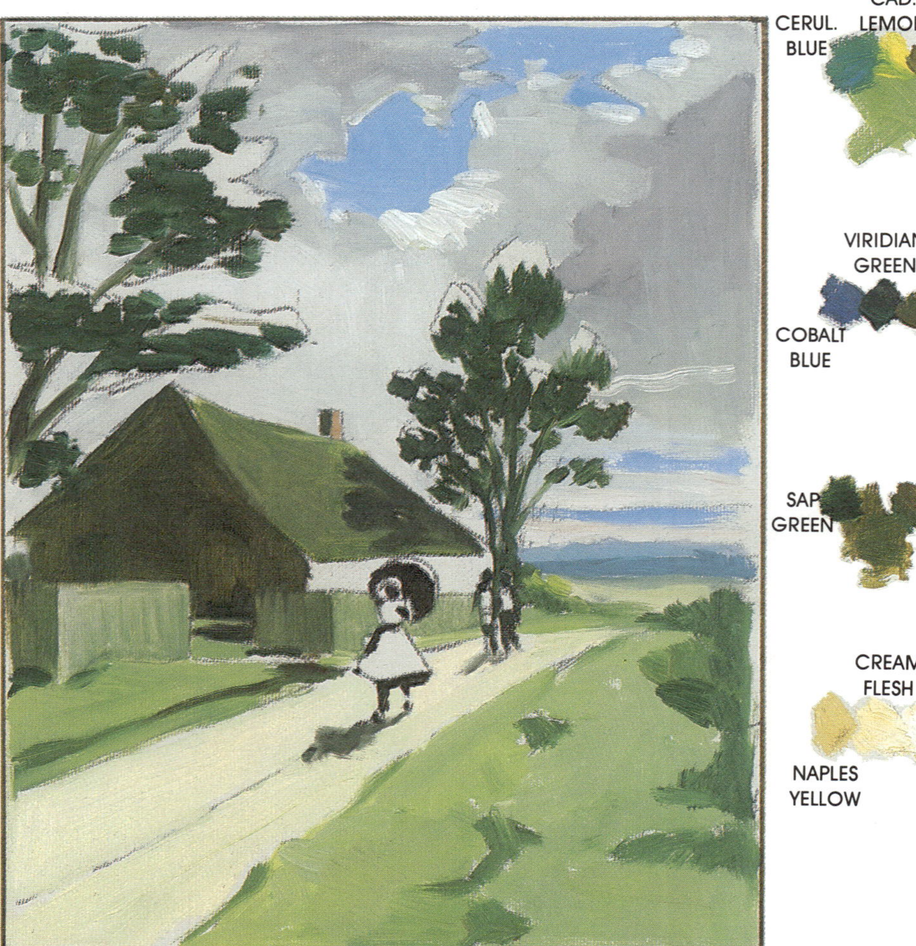

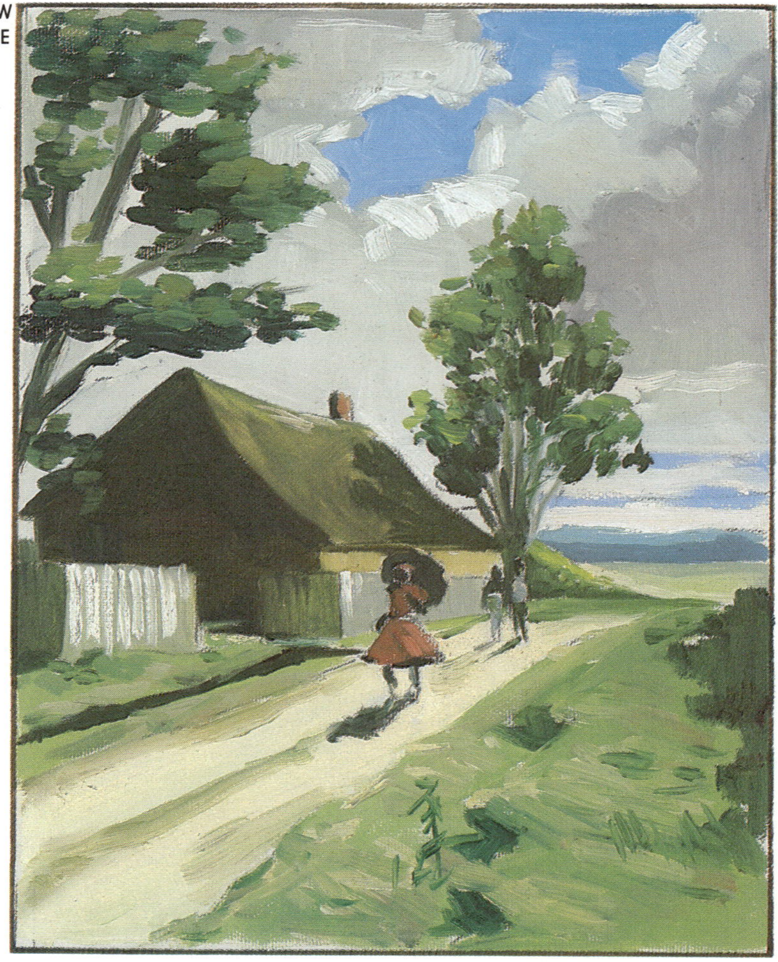

The next step is the house. A mixture of Sap Green and Raw Sienna is used, working dark to light. The leaves on the trees are made with heavy, short strokes. The colors are Cobalt, Viridian, Raw Sienna and White. I now block-in the grass with a green mixture made from Cerulean, Cad. Lemon and Yellow Ochre.

Naples Yellow and White are used for the wall on the house. Naples and Cream Flesh create the road. At this point the painting nears completion. A pointed sable brush and a script brush are used for the detail in the trees and flowers. I break up the green grass with Naples Yellow. Then, with a round sable, I paint in the figures and the fence.

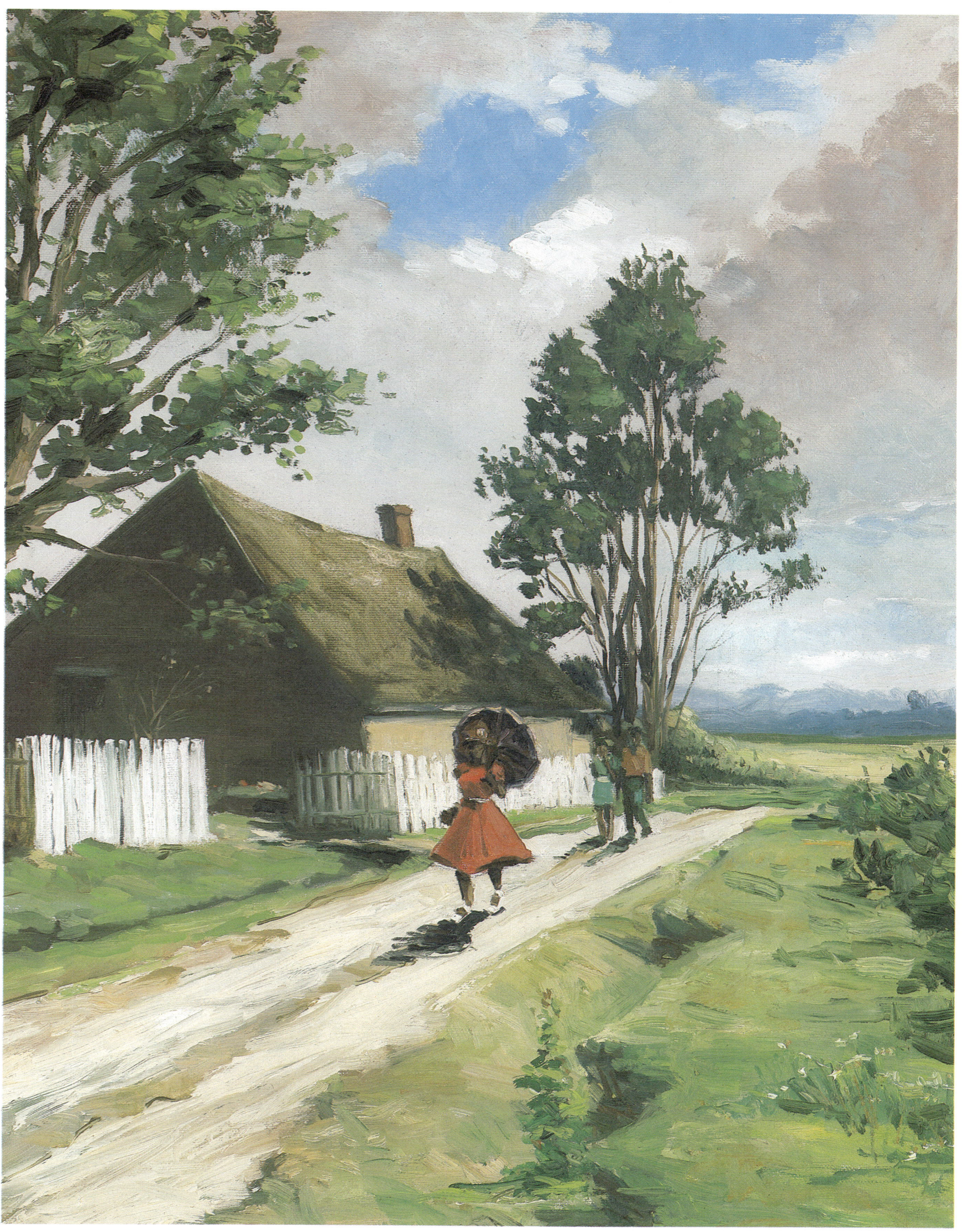

I grew up in the South. Old houses and people walking down dirt roads was a very common sight as a child. Everyday subject matter like this is excellent landscape material. The only difficult part is the main figure. Take a little time and do a few sketches until you feel that it is correct.

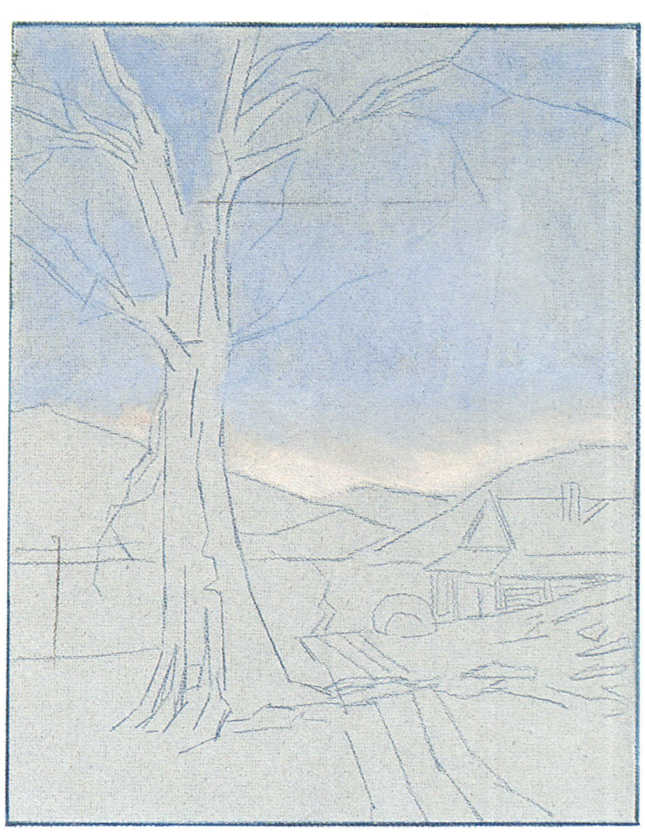

Cobalt Blue and White make up most of the sky. Near the horizon I added Pink Flesh plus a bit of White. This makes for a very interesting effect.

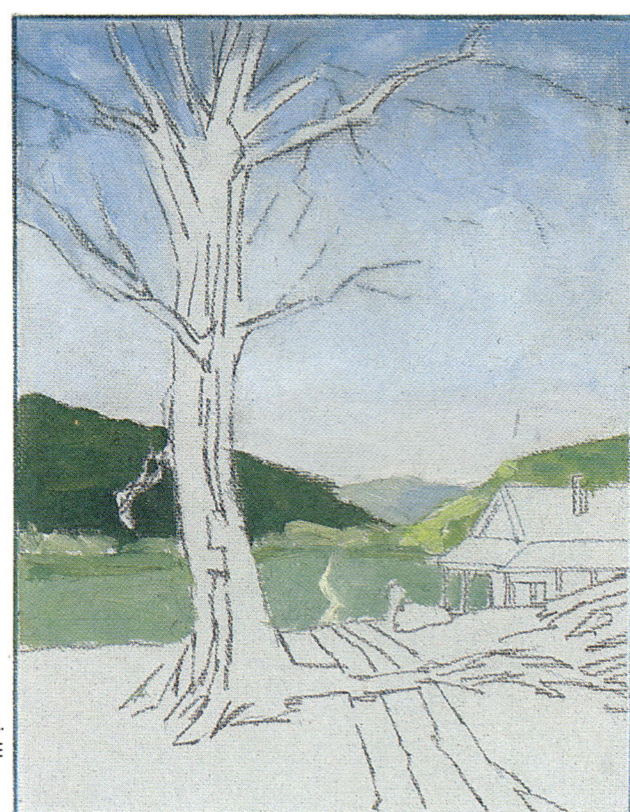

The background is now painted. Pale Blue is used for the most distant mountains, and Viridian and Raw Sienna are used for the mountains on the left. Yellow Ochre, Viridian and Blue are the basic tones on the mountains on the right. Add a little Brilliant Yellow-Green for highlights. Viridian, Blue and a touch of Yellow Ochre make up the middle pasture.

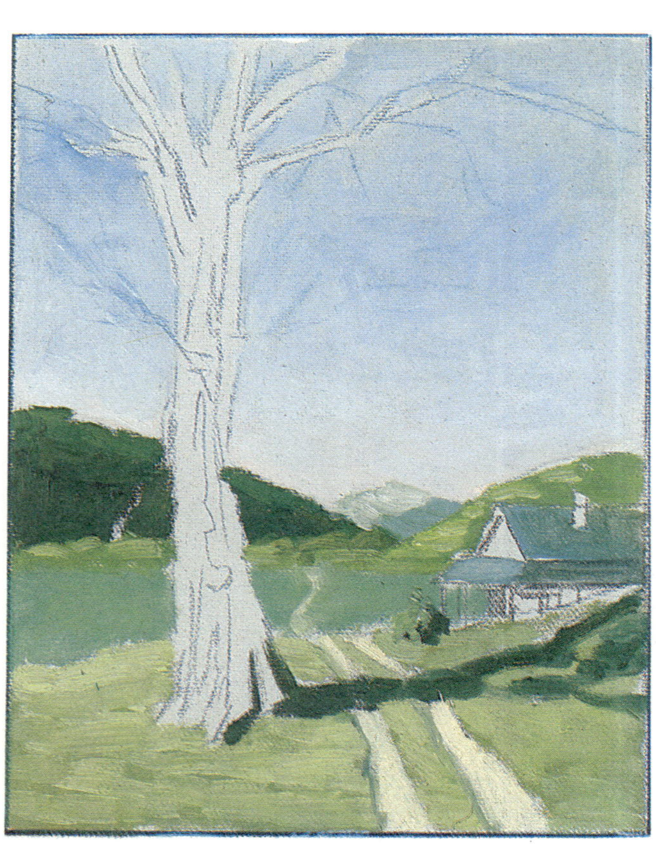

The foreground should be much warmer. To achieve this, mix Brilliant Yellow-Green with small amounts of Raw Sienna. Add more texture by using bristle flats and thicker paint. Mix some Cream Flesh with a touch of Raw Sienna for the road.

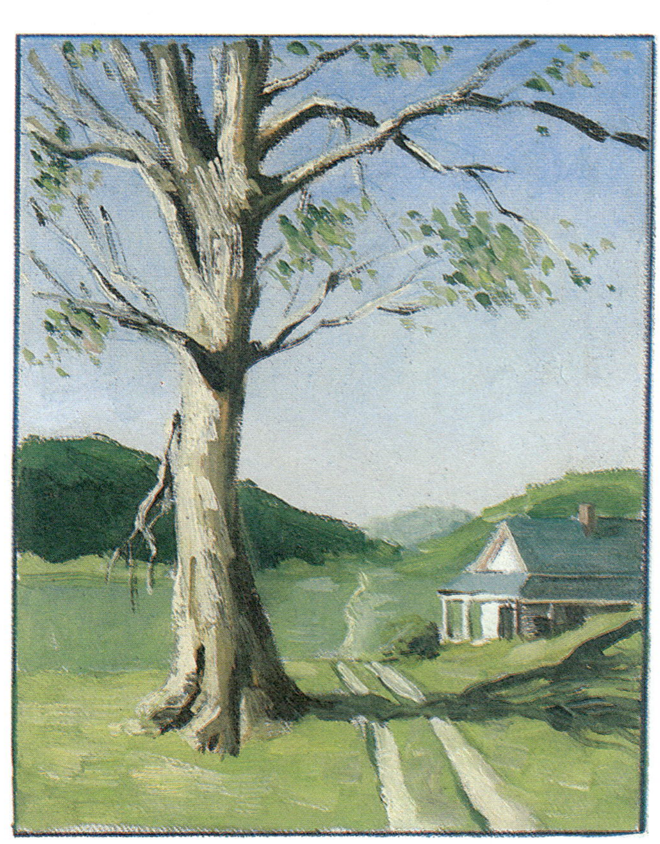

The tree is quite simple. Cad. Red Light and Viridian are mixed to make up the shadows. Cad. Red and Naples Yellow are used for the middle tones. Naples Yellow is the base tone with Cream Flesh for the highlights. I used a sable round to create the leaves. You may have noticed that Pink Flesh was also used to break up the green leaves.

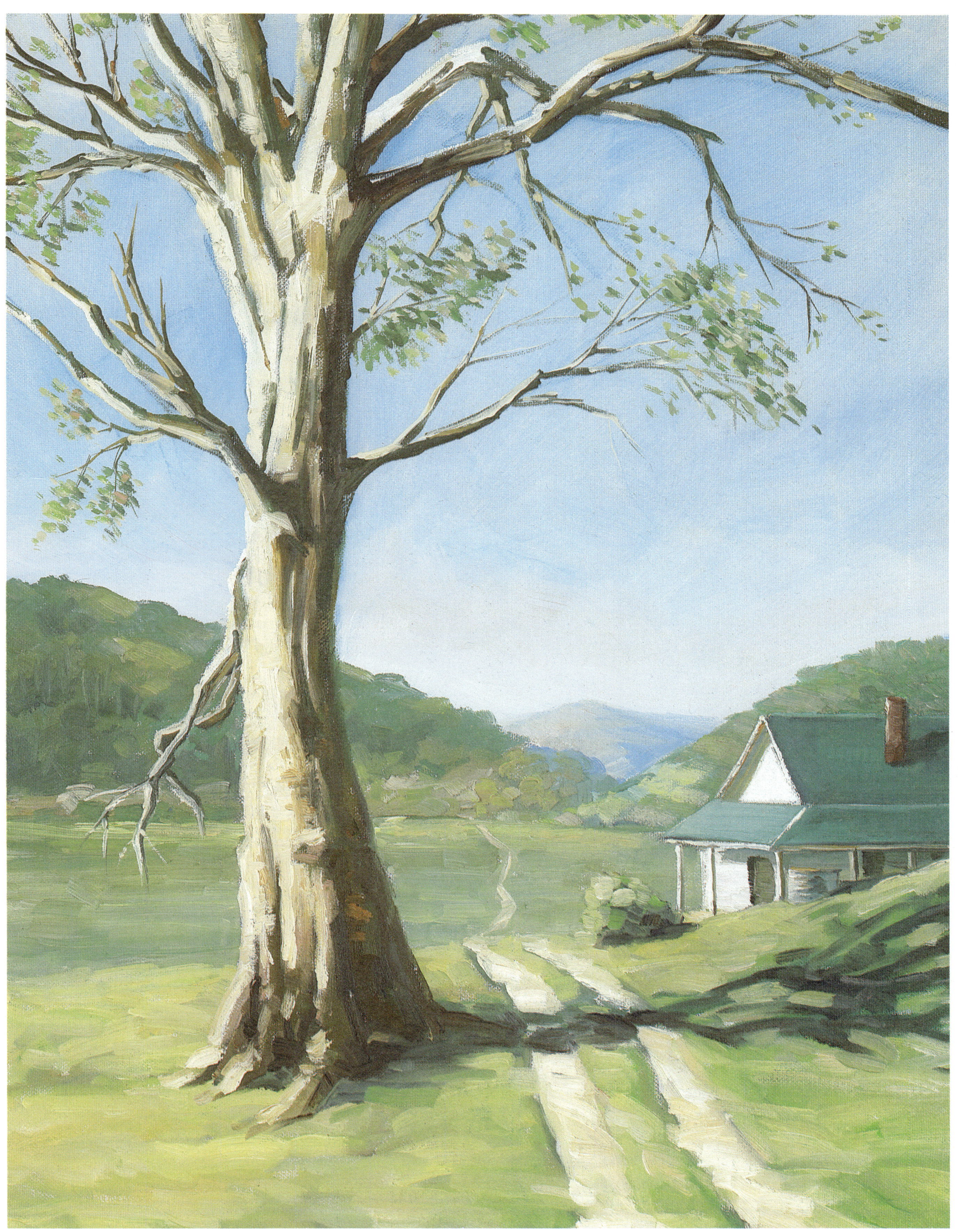

The colors in this painting are very soft. The browns in the tree are made with Green and Orange; this makes them less harsh. The colors are all muted with Cream Flesh or White to create the overall pastel effect.

This is a very special scene to me. I spent most of my teen years in Australia. This is a close reproduction of a farm my family almost bought.

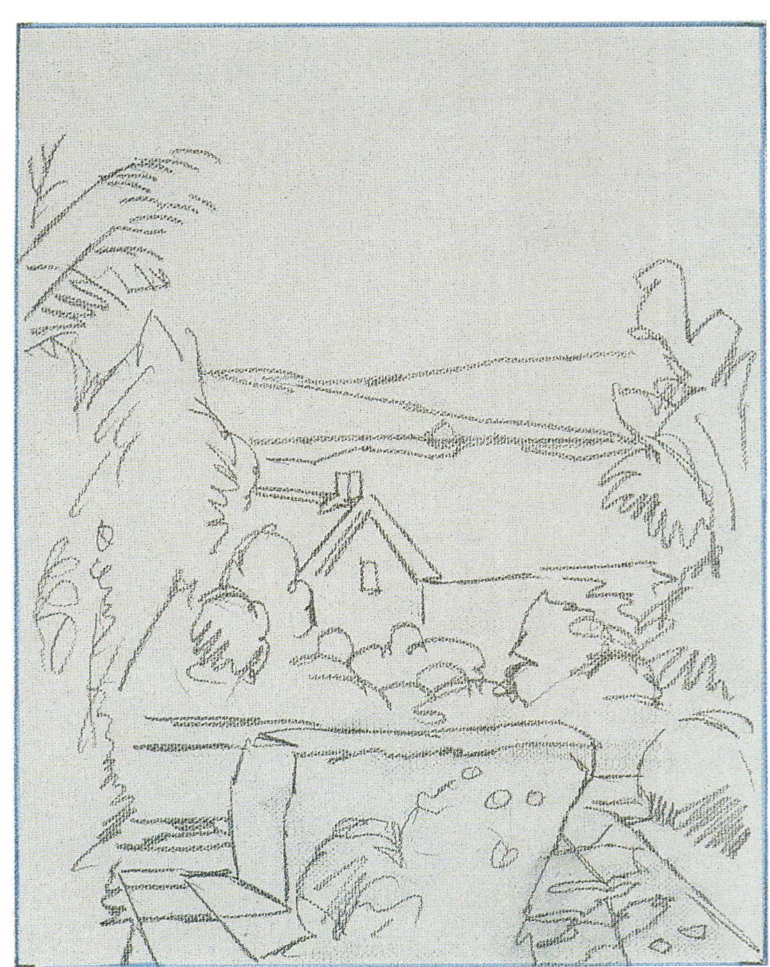

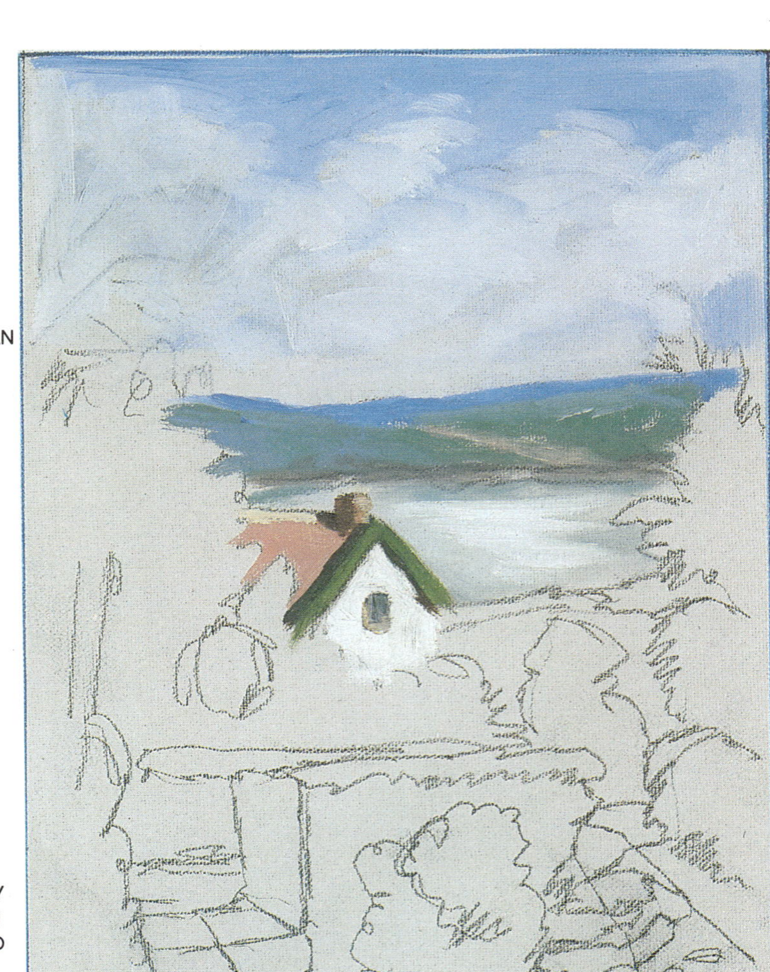

Once again, prepare. Draw as detailed a sketch as you feel necessary. Use pencil or paint with a round sable brush (whichever you feel most comfortable with).

By now you should have the hang of it. Cobalt Blue and White in the sky, and Cobalt, Cerulean and a touch of Yellow Ochre comprise the distant hills. Traditional Flesh and a touch of Cream Flesh are all that are used for the tile-like roof.

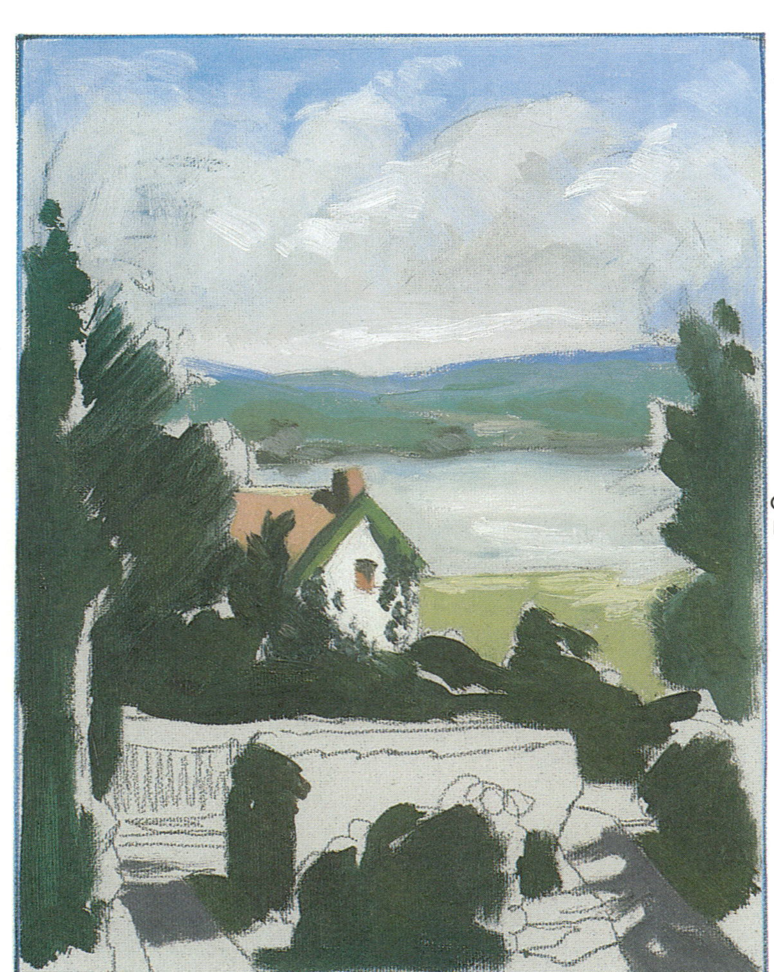

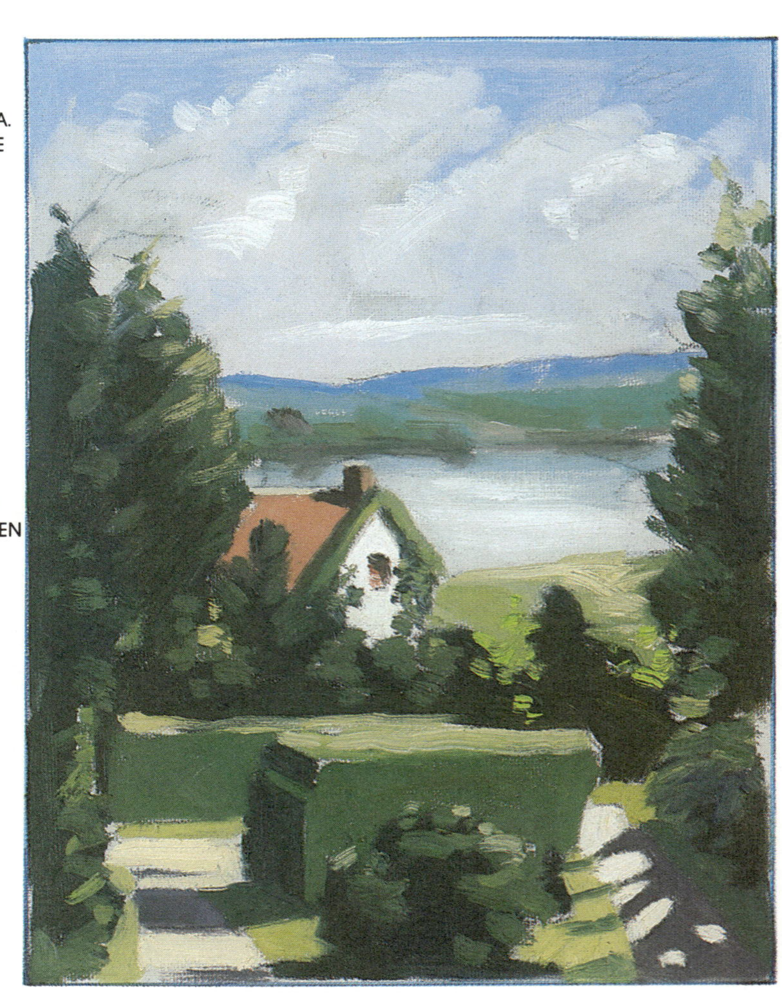

Viridian Green and Ultramarine Blue are used for the darkest values. The light green grass is a mixture of Brilliant Yellow-Green, Cad. Yellow Medium and Traditional Flesh. The pathway shadows are created with a mixture of the Violets. The highlights on the path are straight Traditional Flesh.

As I near completion I am only concerned with the light areas and the dark shadows. This is a very thick painting and I used only bristle brushes. Even in the final stage, I used loaded round bristles to create the texture and the roses.

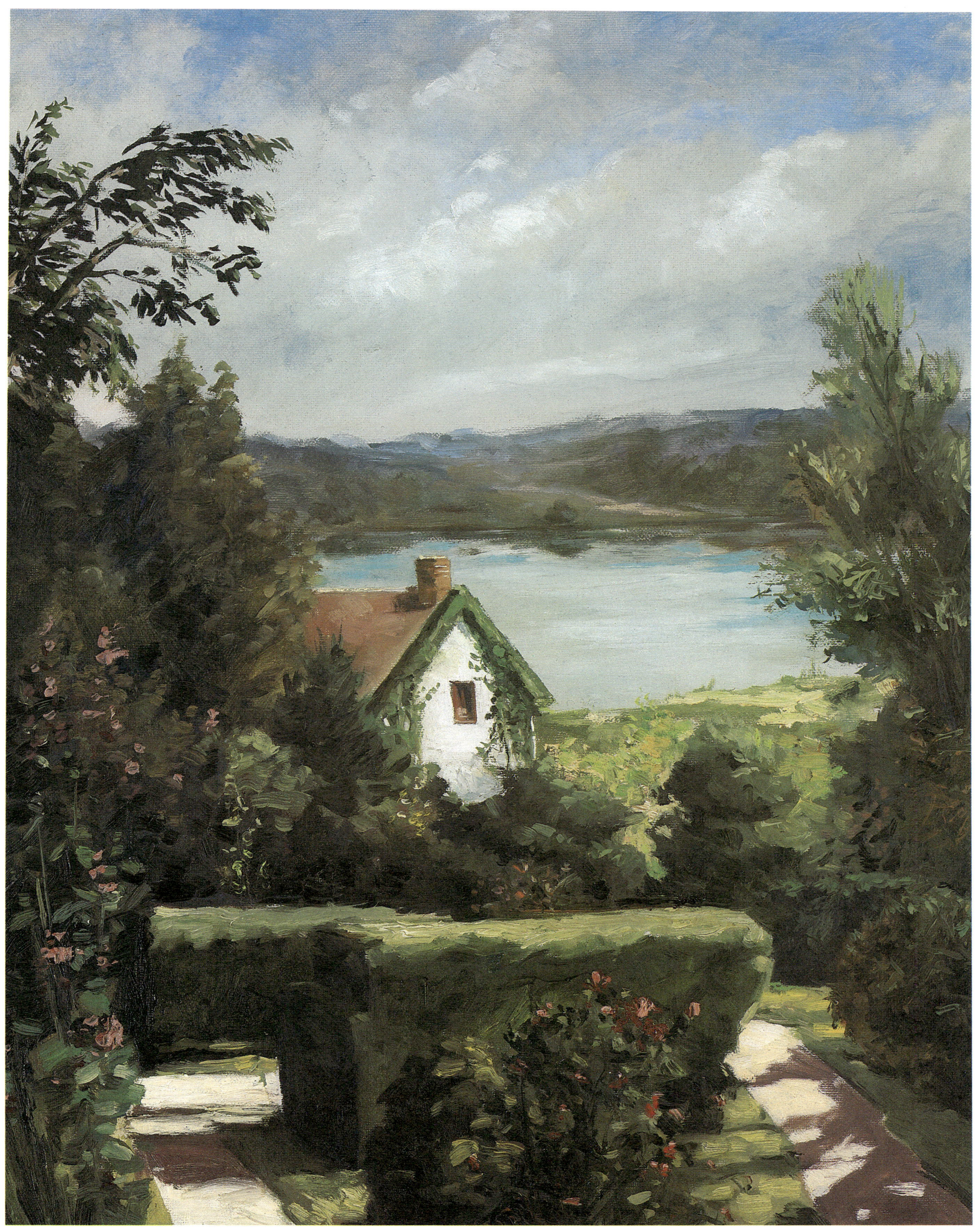

Houses wtih gardens are great fun to paint. There are many simple shapes such as rectangle hedges and the triangles of the roof. The key to painting a scene like this is to draw the shapes and block-in the darks and lights. If you squint your eyes the values are easy to make out. I squint a lot while painting.

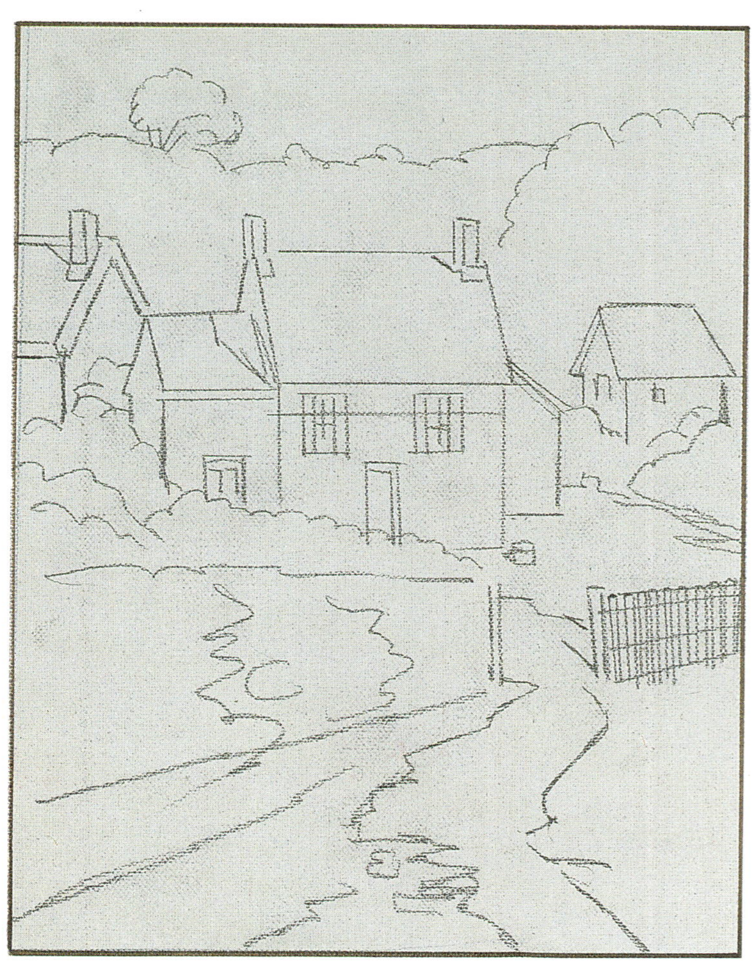

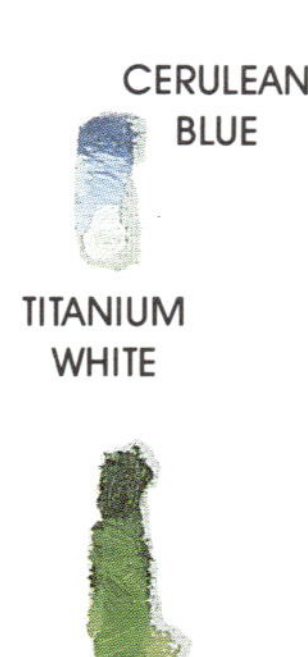

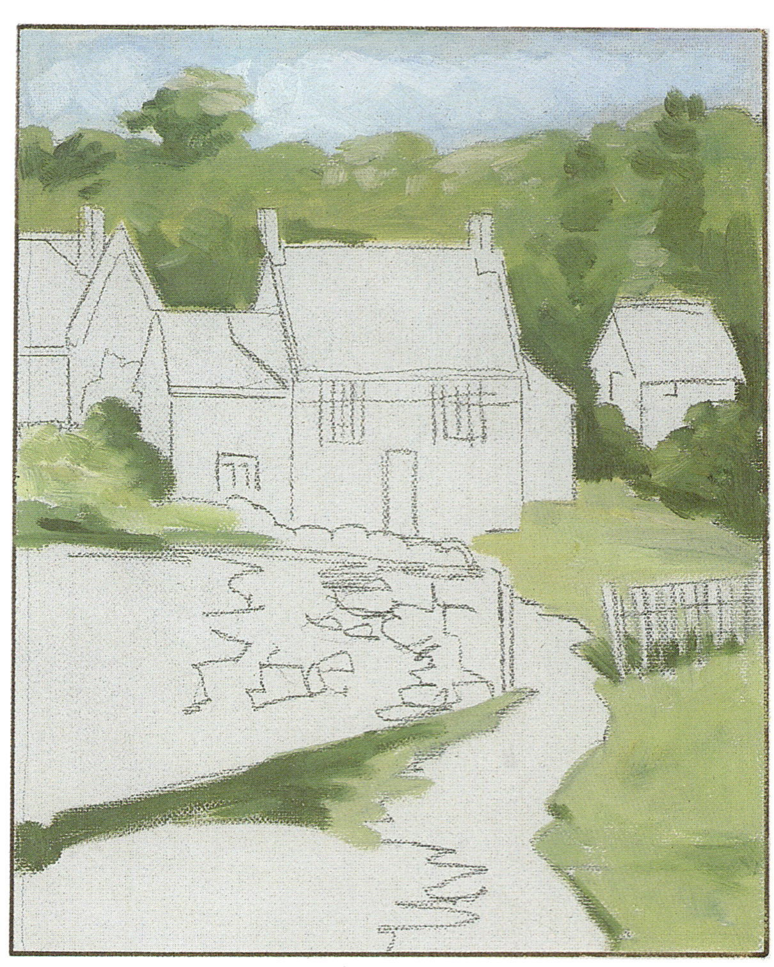

AFTER YOU HAVE COMPLETED YOUR DRAWING, BLOCK-IN THE MAJOR AREAS WITH THE COLORS ABOVE. PAINT RATHER THICKLY. USE SHORT STROKES IN THE DARK AREAS TO CREATE TEXTURE.

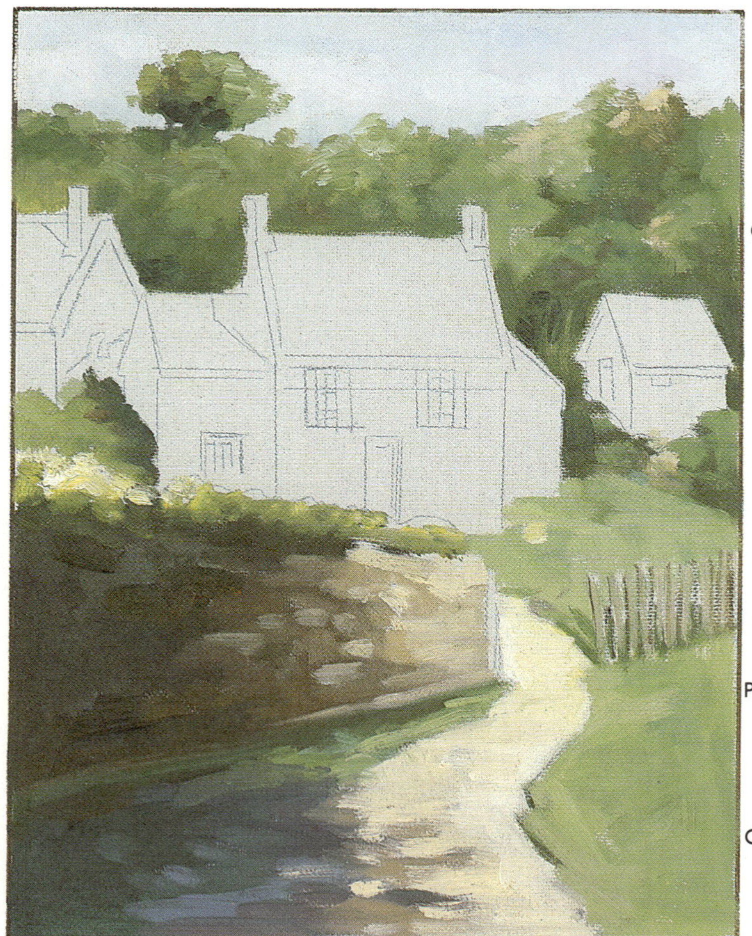

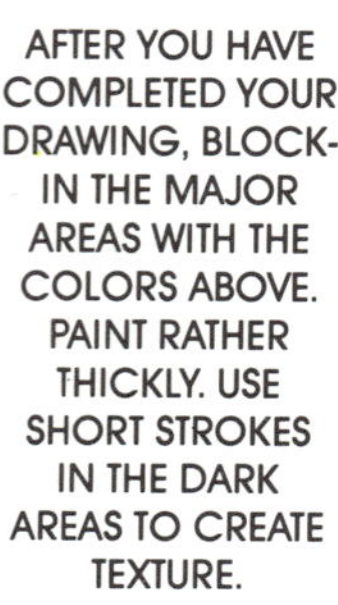

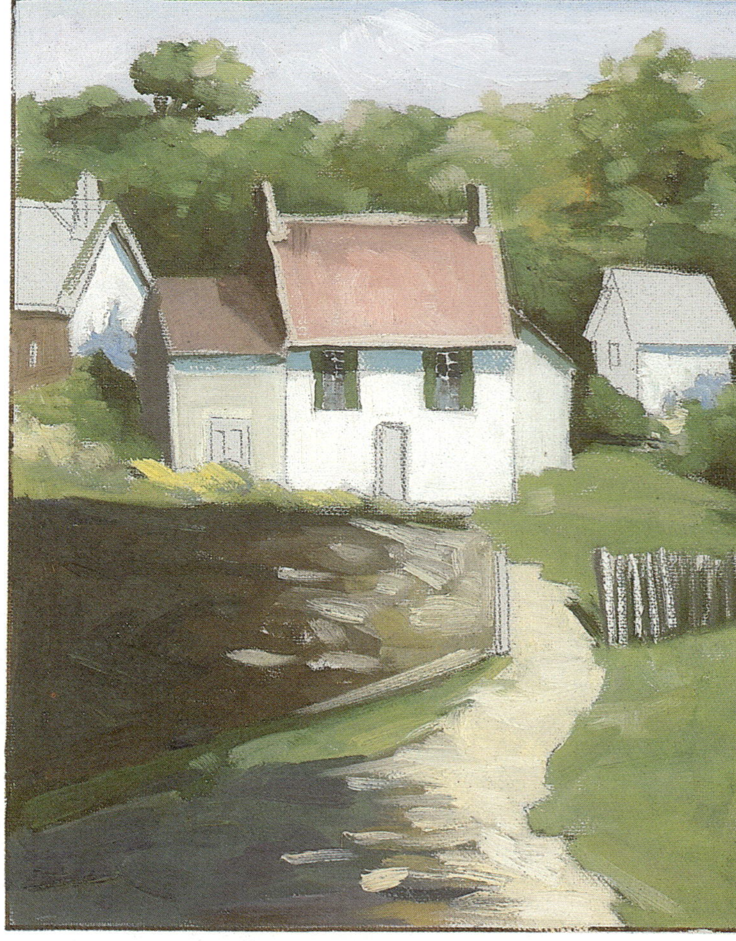

Mix Ultramarine Blue with Orange to create the dark and middle values of the wall. Take some of your Cream Flesh and indicate stones in the wall. Then, using the same color, paint in the pathway. The shadows falling on the path are a mixture of Ultra. Blue and Rose Madder (Violet).

Mars Violet and Cadmium Red Light are used for the dark roofs and Cadmium Red Light and Pink are used for the center and left roofs. The stucco walls are Off White and Pure White. The shadows are Cerulean Blue. I switched to a round sable and dragged White over the grayish fence to create the picket fence effect.

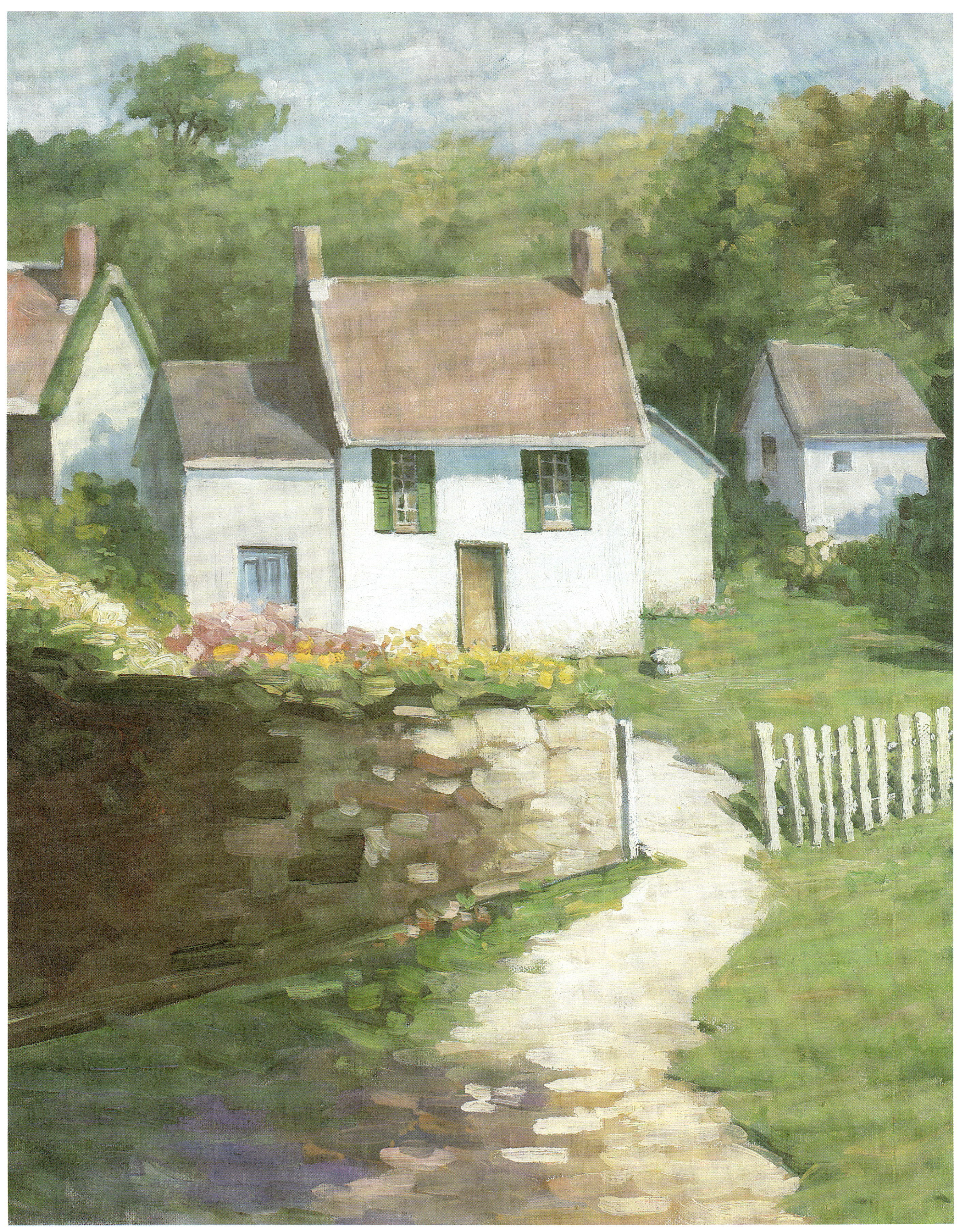

English cottages are a favorite subject. Green grass and pink roofs just seem to go together. Note, there are **no browns** in this painting. The predominant colors are Purples, Pinks, Greens, Blues, Creams and White. I have made extensive use of Pink and the two flesh colors on my palette to paint the roofs.

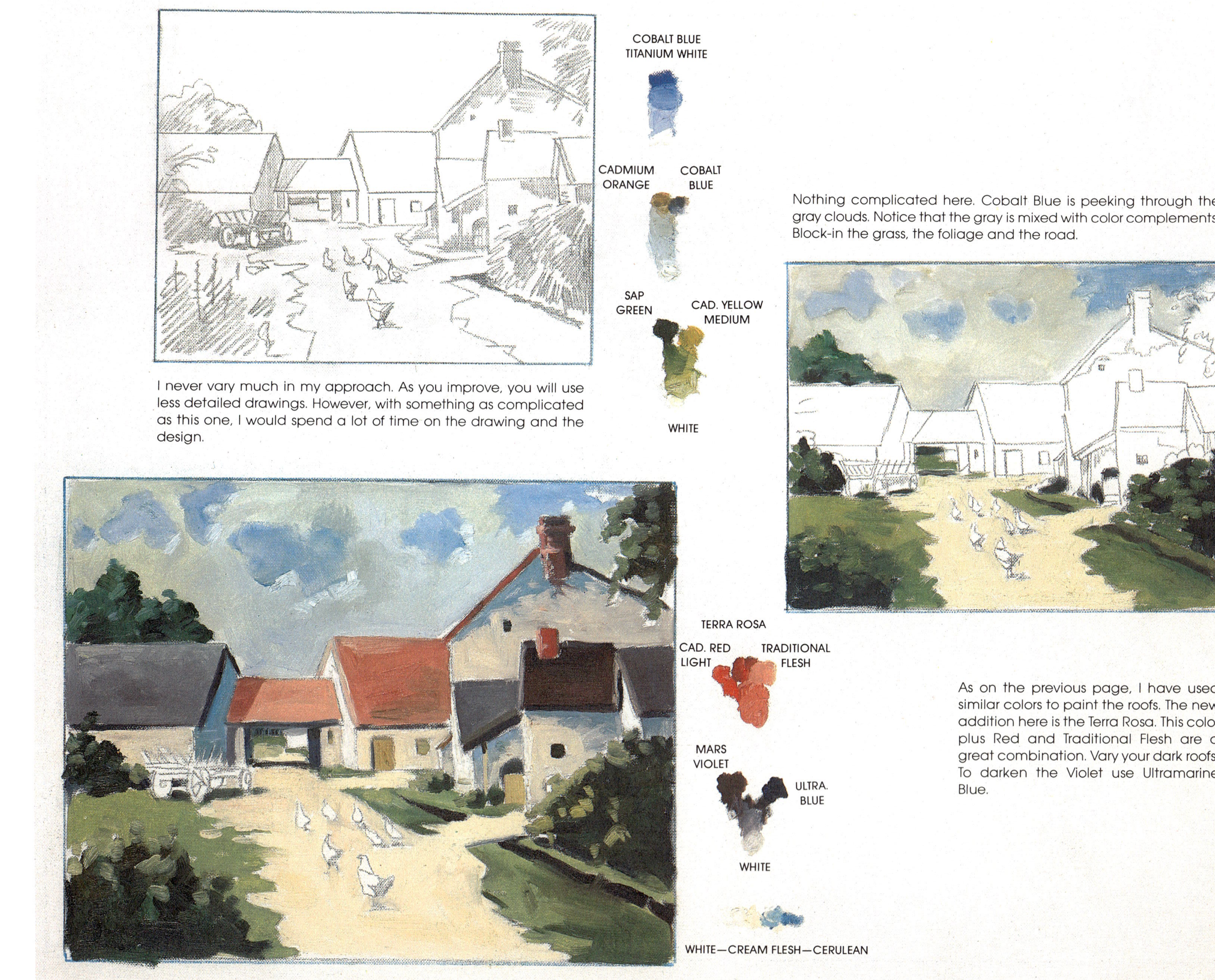

I never vary much in my approach. As you improve, you will use less detailed drawings. However, with something as complicated as this one, I would spend a lot of time on the drawing and the design.

Nothing complicated here. Cobalt Blue is peeking through the gray clouds. Notice that the gray is mixed with color complements. Block-in the grass, the foliage and the road.

As on the previous page, I have used similar colors to paint the roofs. The new addition here is the Terra Rosa. This color plus Red and Traditional Flesh are a great combination. Vary your dark roofs. To darken the Violet use Ultramarine Blue.

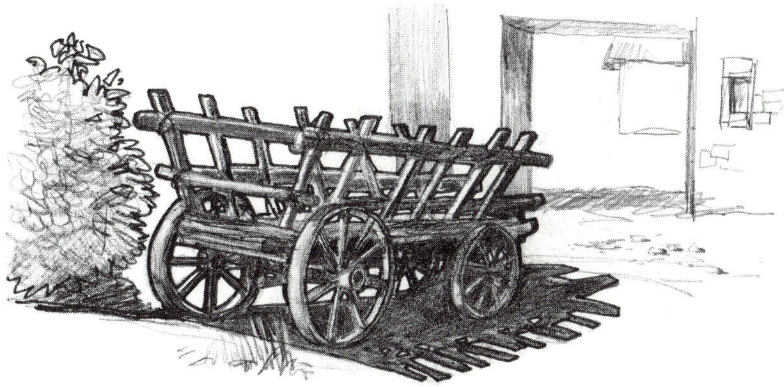

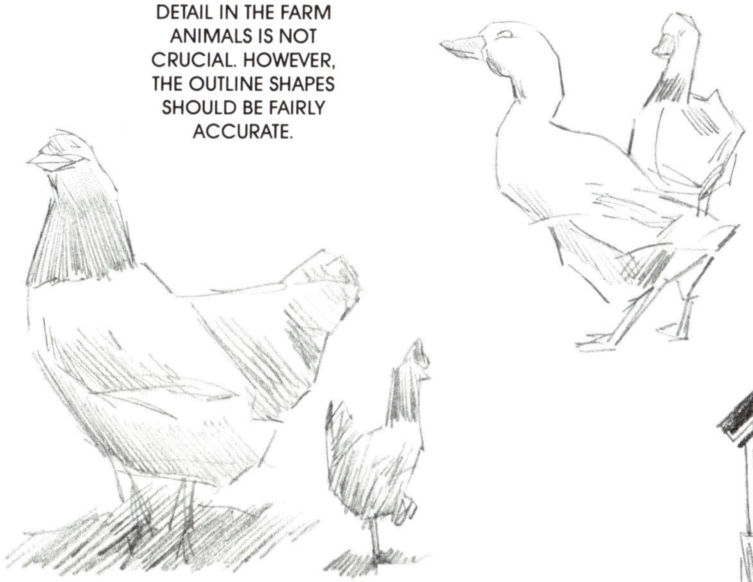

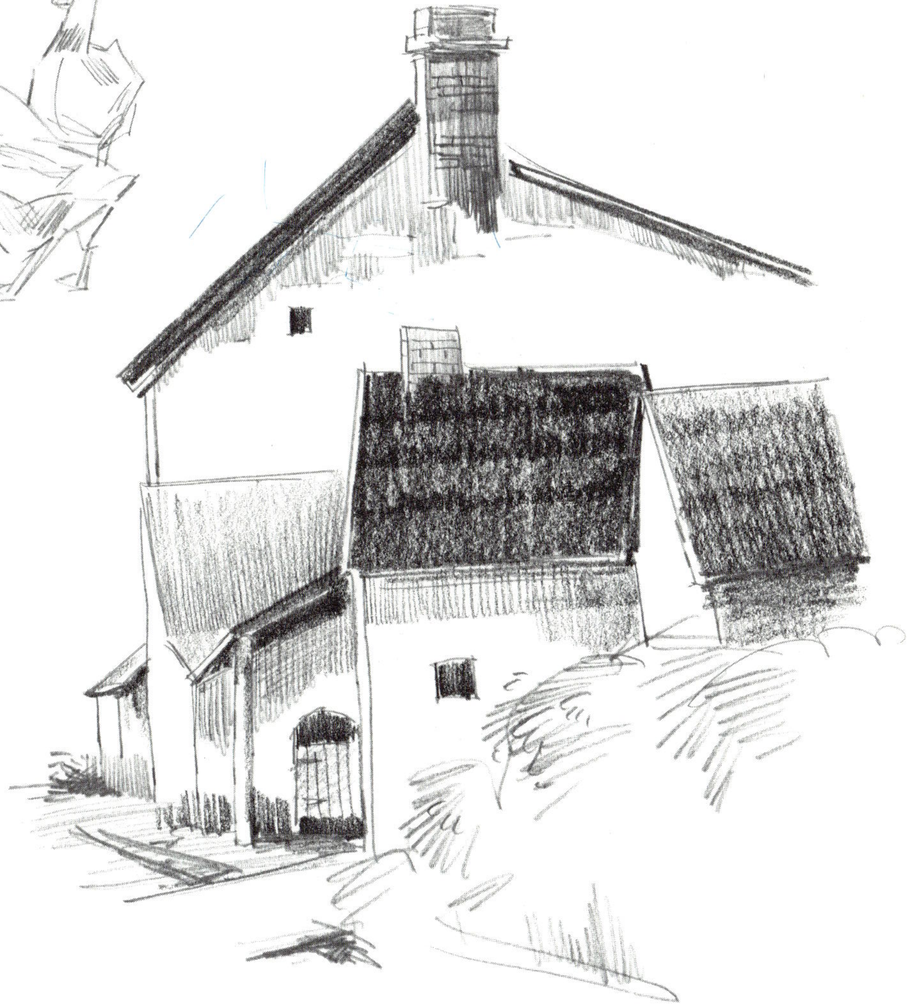

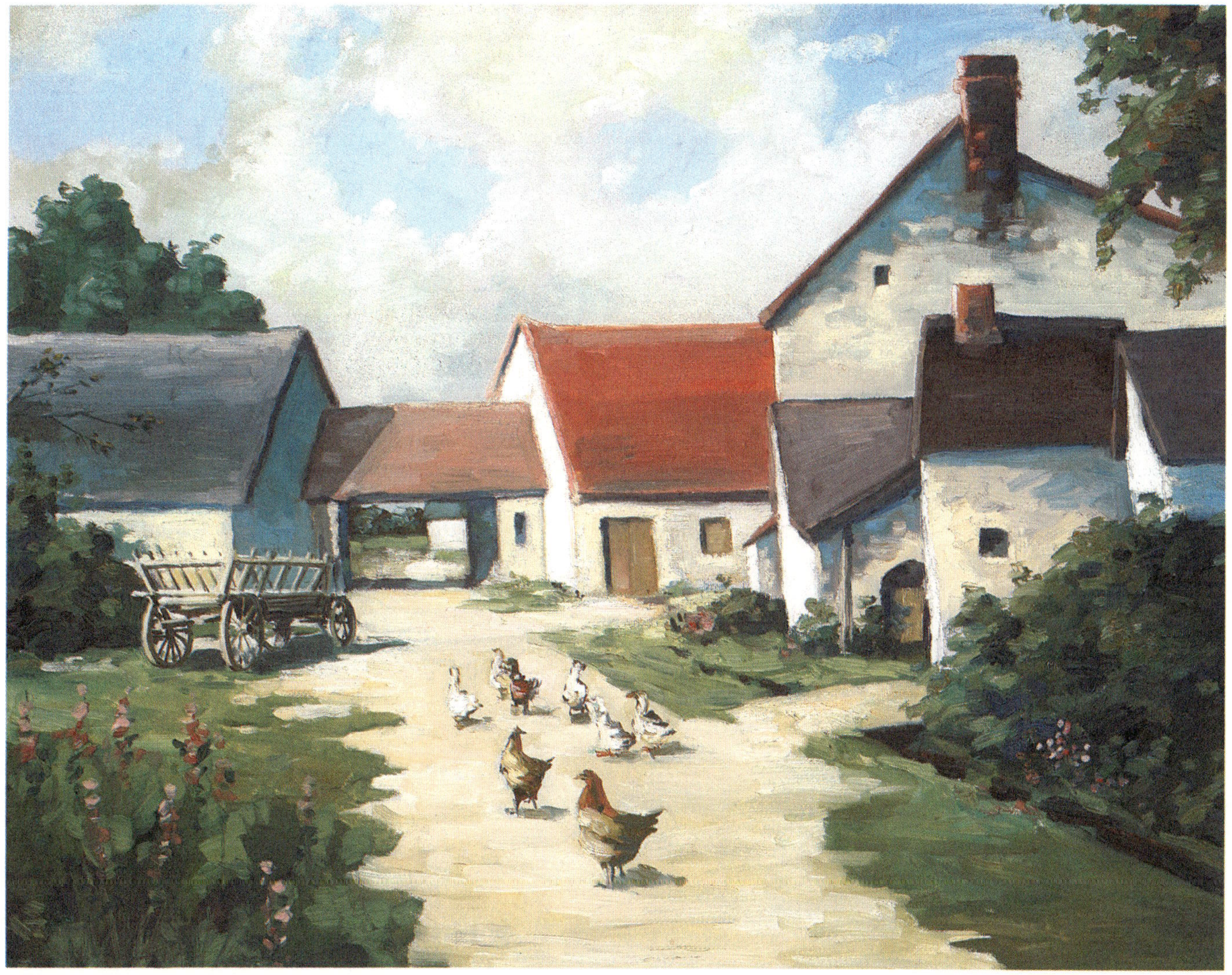

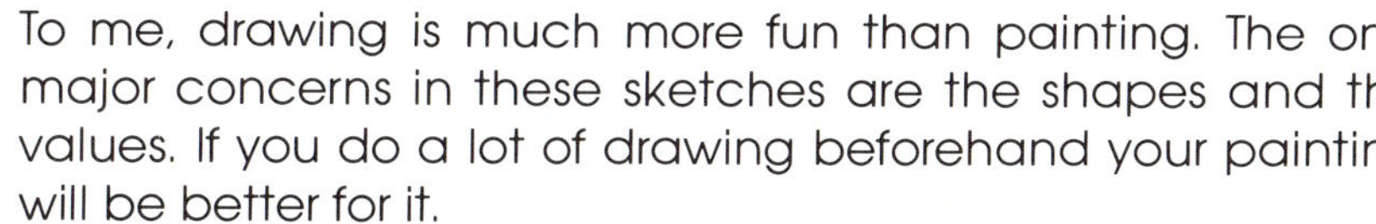

To me, drawing is much more fun than painting. The only major concerns in these sketches are the shapes and the values. If you do a lot of drawing beforehand your painting will be better for it.

This landscape has a European flavor. In Europe farm buildings are built close together and often share a common wall. The groupings lend themselves to an interesting combination.

What farm scene would be complete without an old wagon and some farm animals? A lot of detail is not necessary to convey these elements, however, take care in your drawings to insure believability.

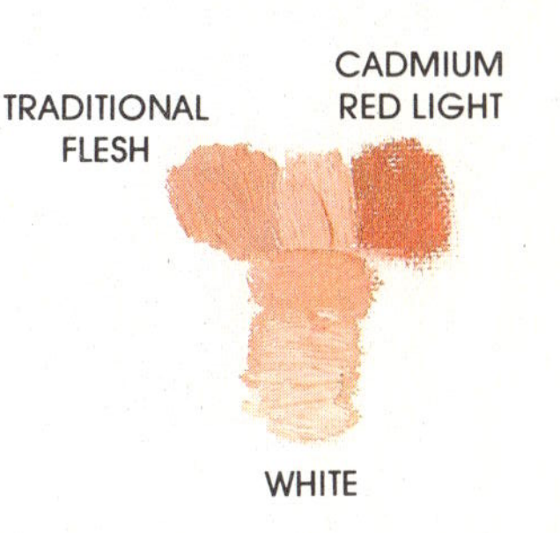

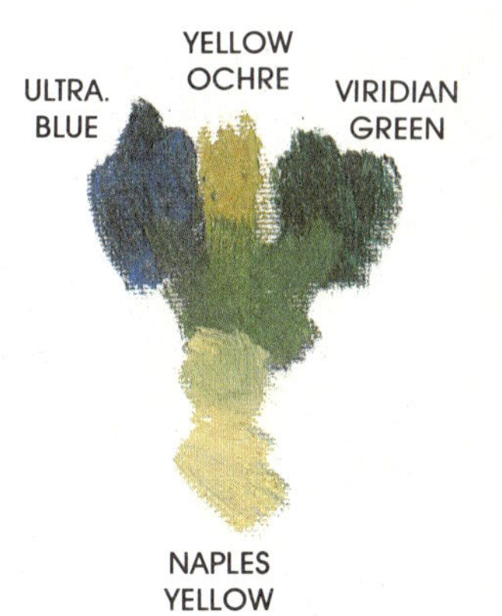

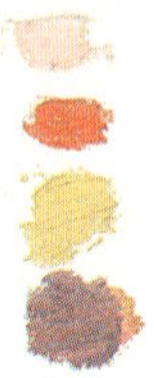

Every now and then it is fun to "play" impressionist. Lots of broken color and thick paint give this painting its interest. I used Pinks, Blues, Purples and Greens only.

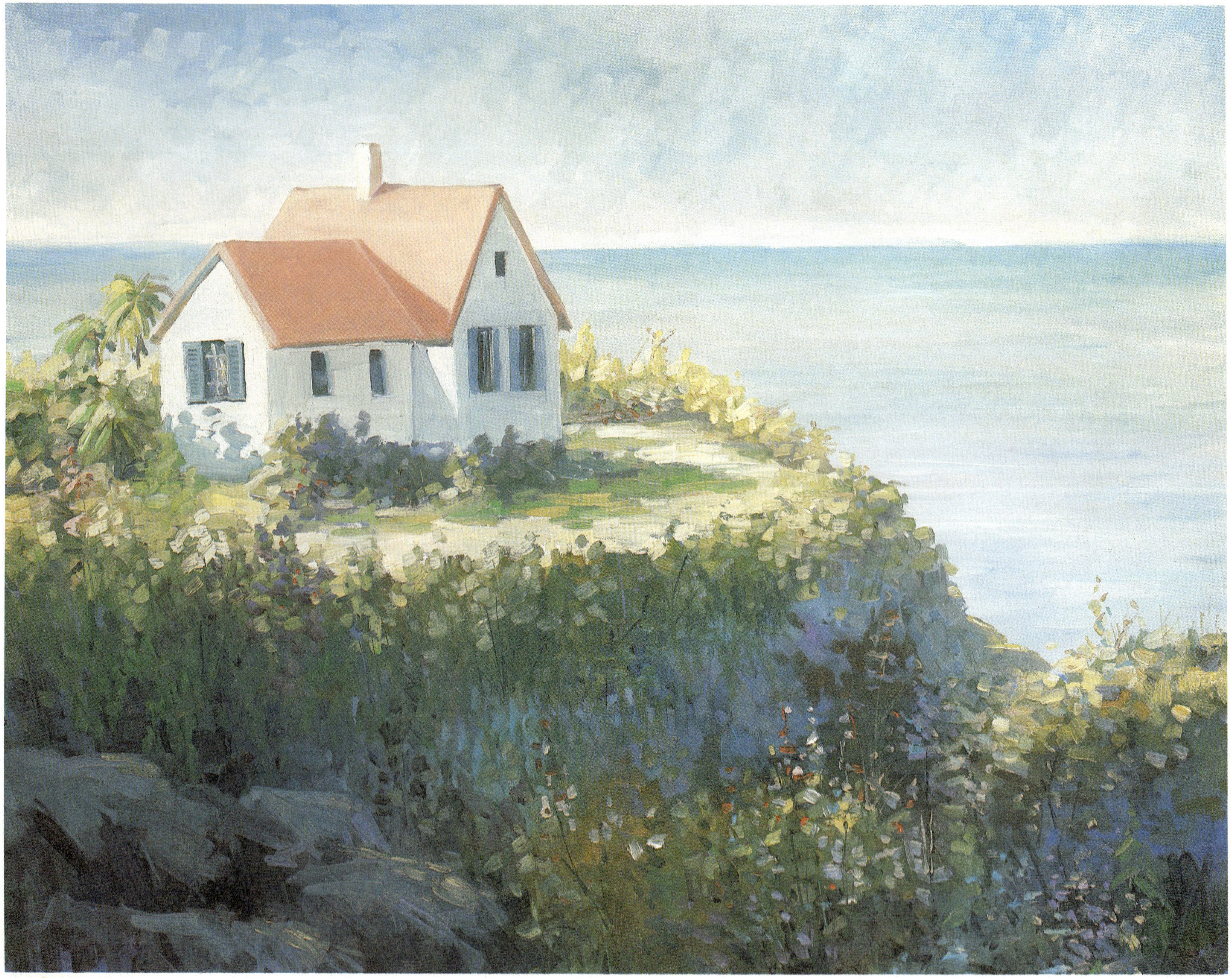

Monet painted a house on a cliff overlooking the ocean. So have I, along with a thousand other artists. Why not join the club?

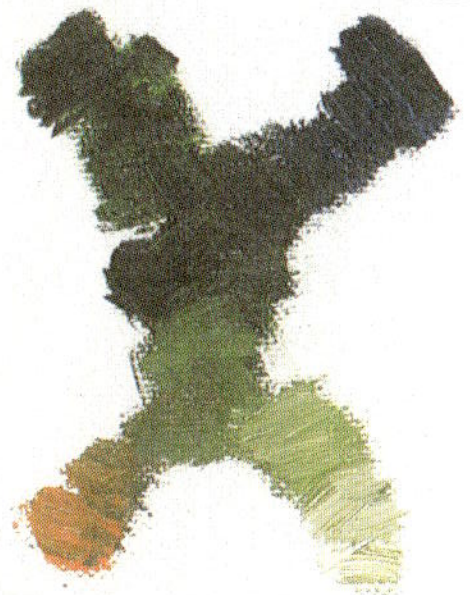

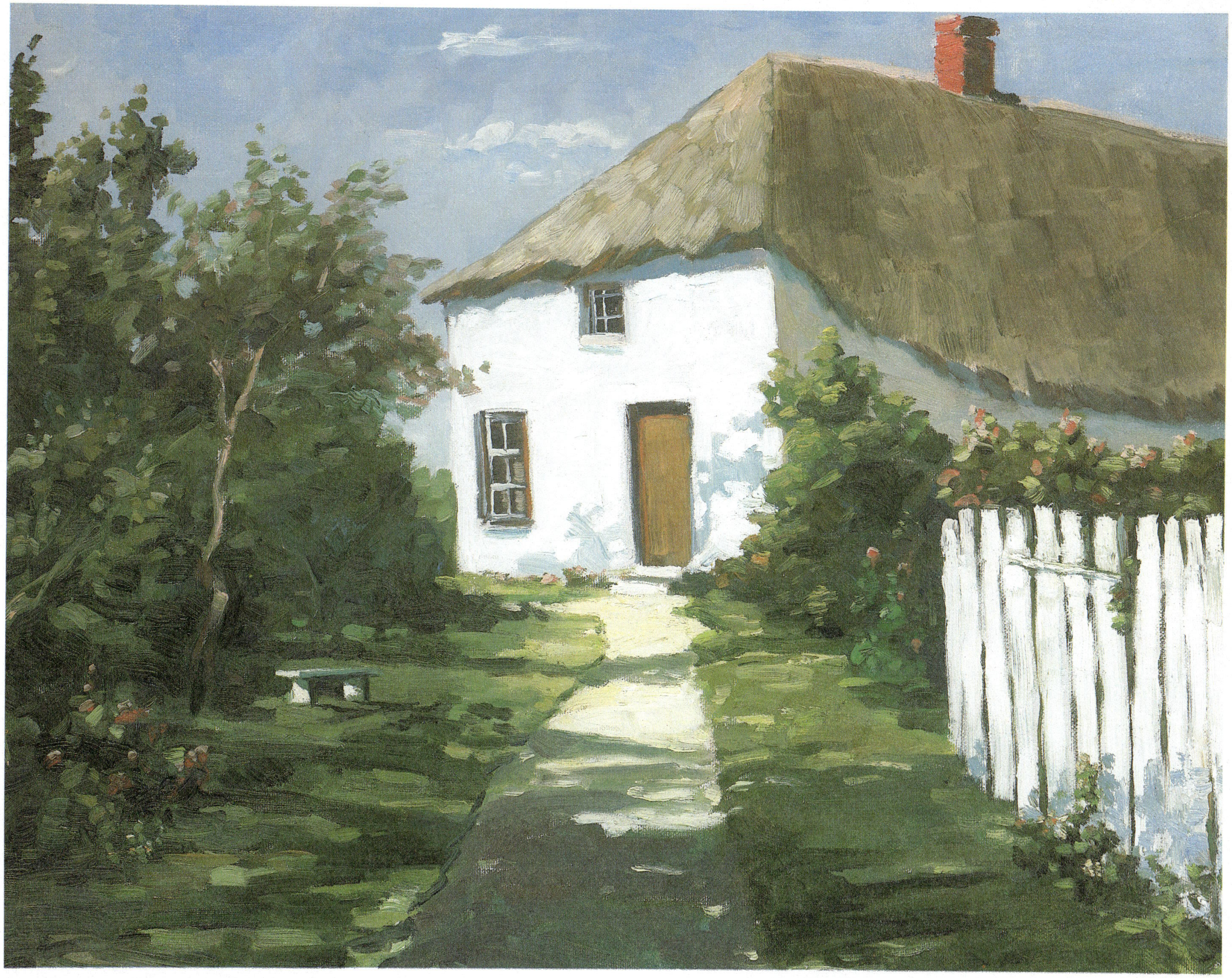

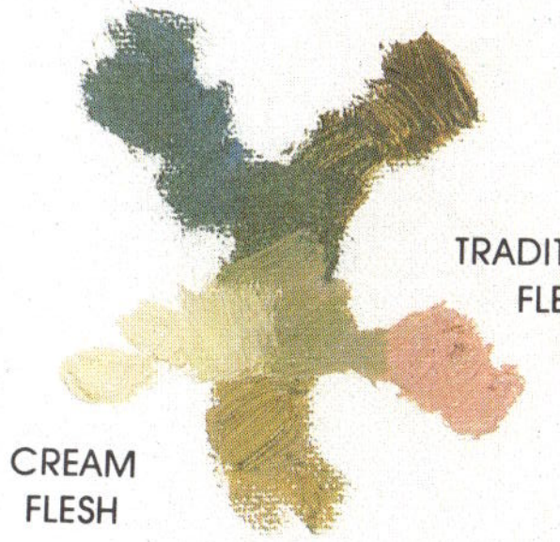

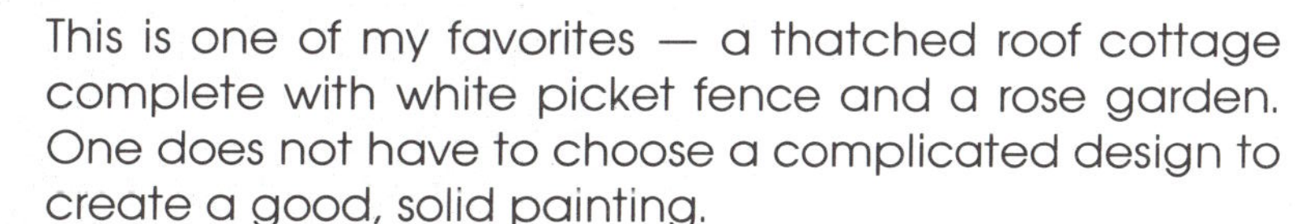

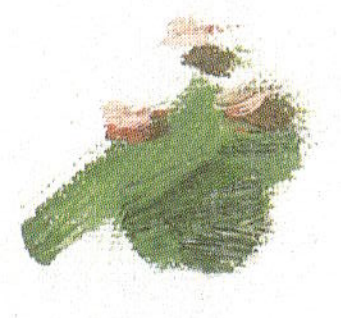

This is one of my favorites — a thatched roof cottage complete with white picket fence and a rose garden. One does not have to choose a complicated design to create a good, solid painting.

My wife, Terri, watched me paint this one. She thought it strange that I would paint the shadows on the house before I painted the trees that create the shadows.

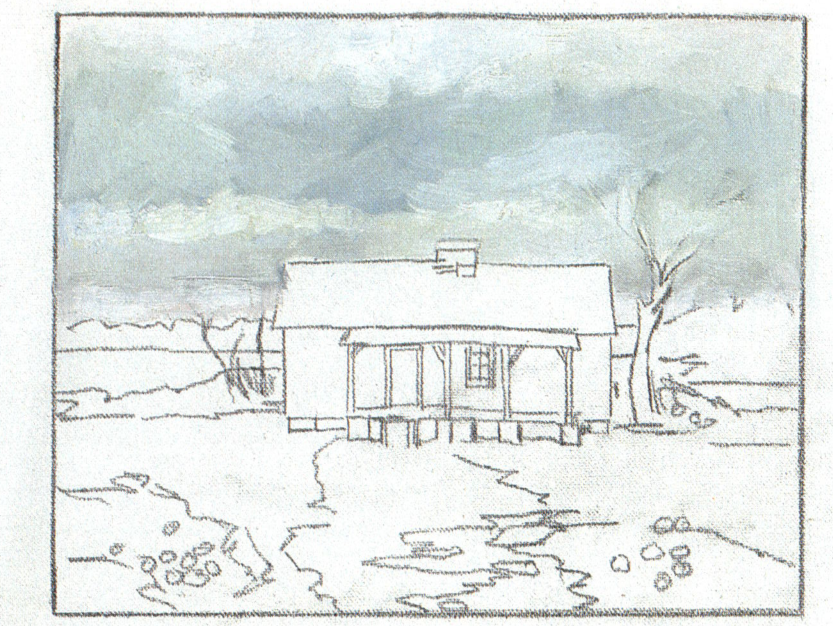

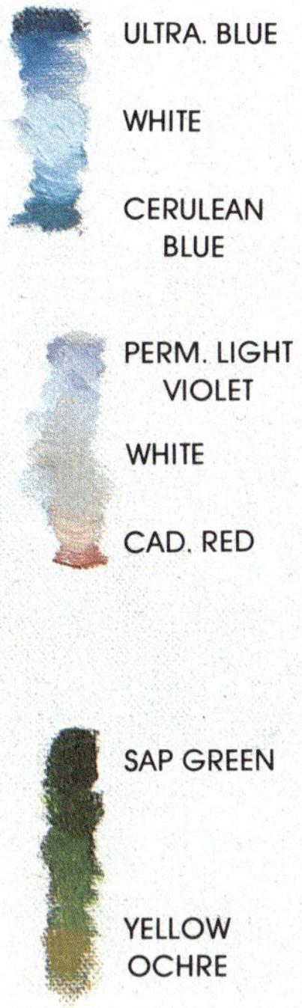

Here I have combined the first two steps. I start with a comprehensive pencil drawing of all the important shapes, then spray it with workable fixative so it doesn't smear. Then, I paint the sky. Two-thirds of the upper sky is painted with Ultramarine and Cerulean. When I near the horizon I add Violet and Pink.

Although the sky was painted with a bristle brush and thick paint, the land and the house are painted with a bright sable using thinner washes. I used Sap Green and Yellow Ochre for the trees and the grass. The roof is painted first with a mixture of Cadmium Orange and a touch of Sap Green. A wash of Viridian is used to block-in the house.

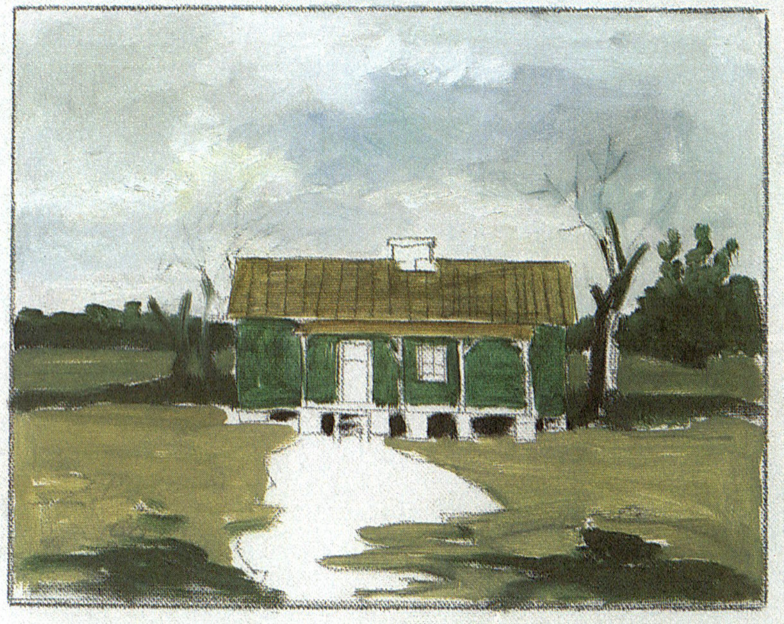

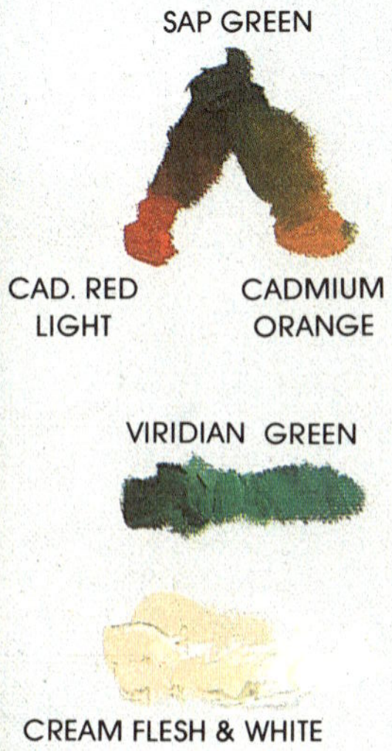

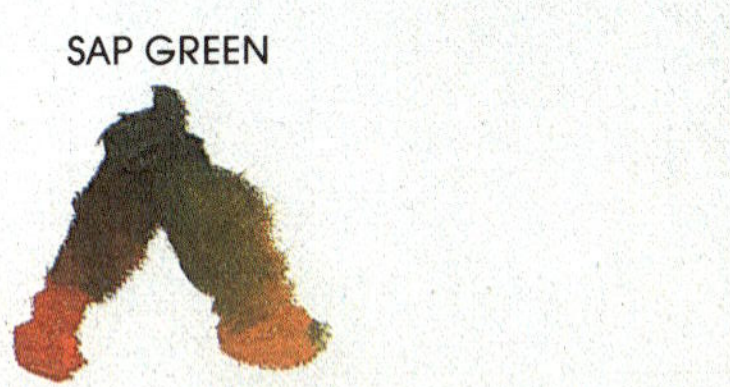

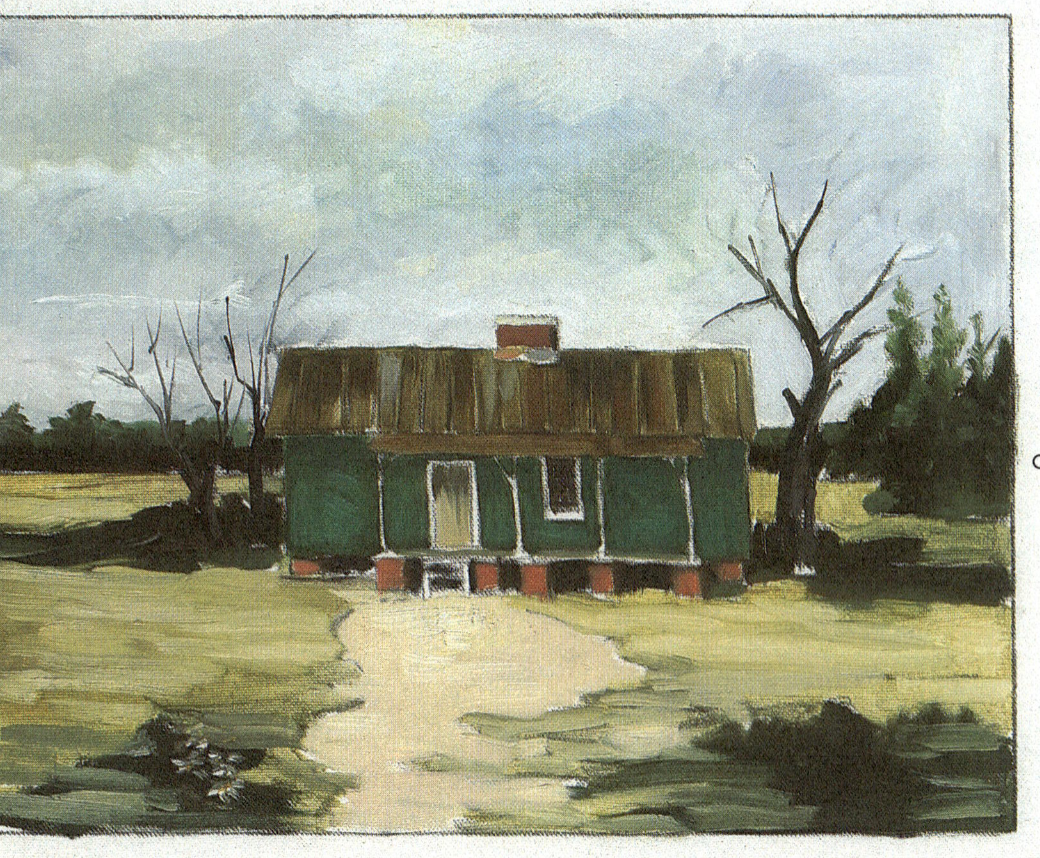

Use the Flesh color with a touch of Cad. Red Light for the dirt path in front of the house. Next, take a bristle flat brush and load it with a mixture of Cad. Red Light and Sap Green. Draw the color down in vertical rows to create the ruts in the roof. The bricks are Cad. Red Light, full strength, with Sap Green added for the shadows. A touch of White is mixed with the Viridian and painted thickly on the walls of the house. A script brush is now employed to paint the details of the trees and the weeds.

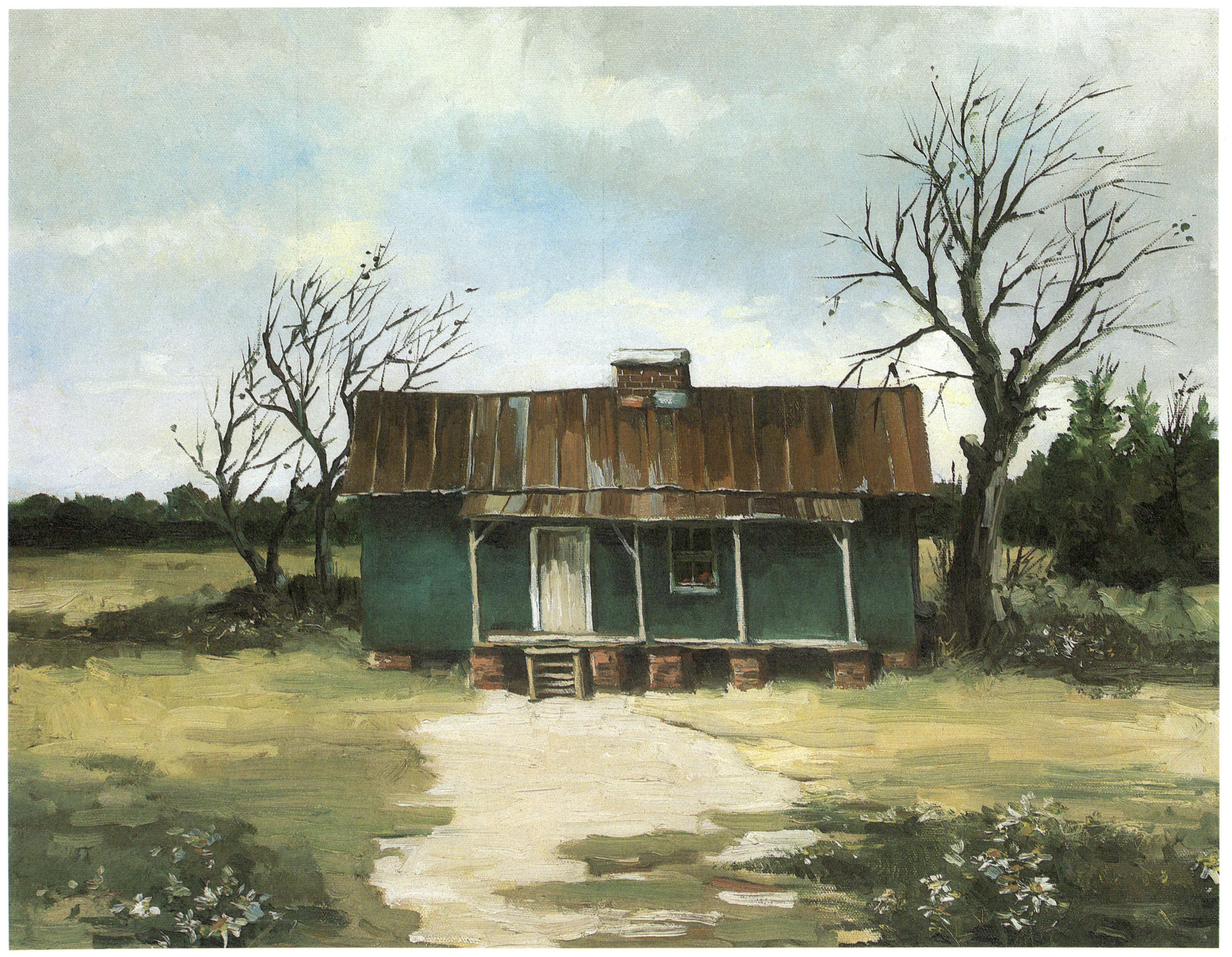

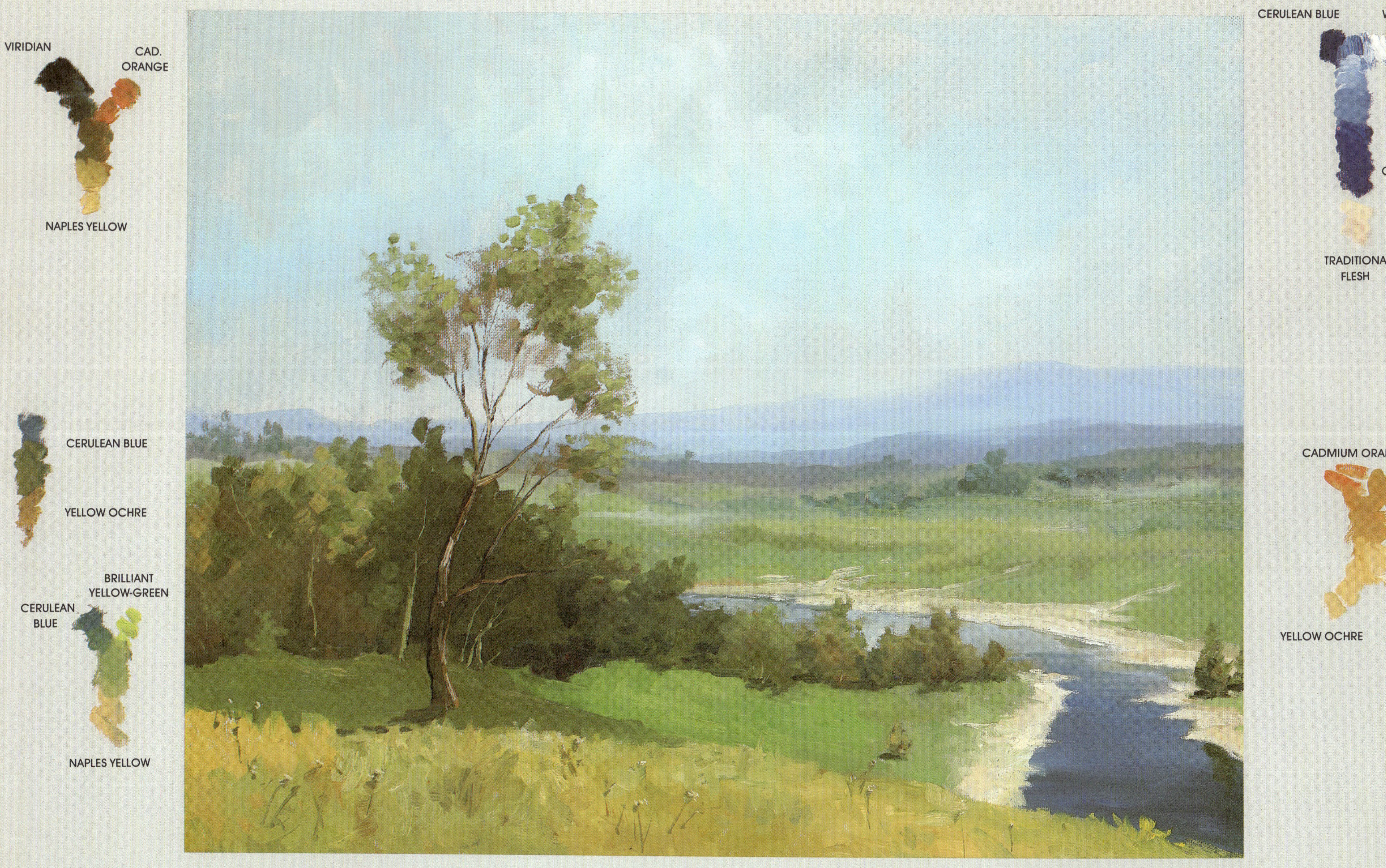

This is another landscape with muted pastel colors. The major interest here is the perspective. Most landscape painters overlook this dramatic view point. The creamy colored shores really work well against the brilliant blues in the river. Also, note the old adage — warm colors come forward and cool colors recede.

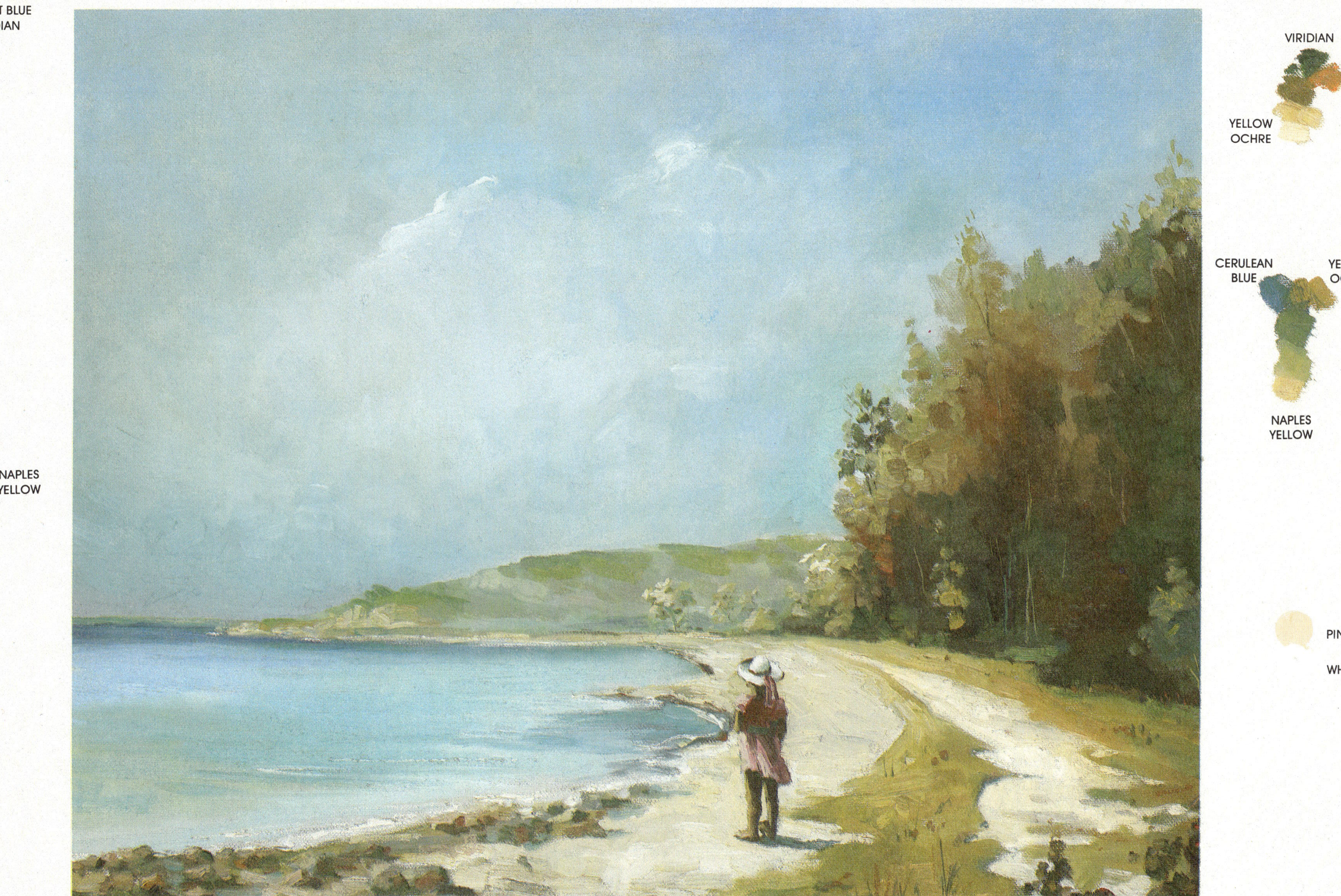

Although this painting has a very simple composition, it does retain a certain drama. The single figure here conveys a lonely theme. The last day at the lake or the end of summer perhaps?

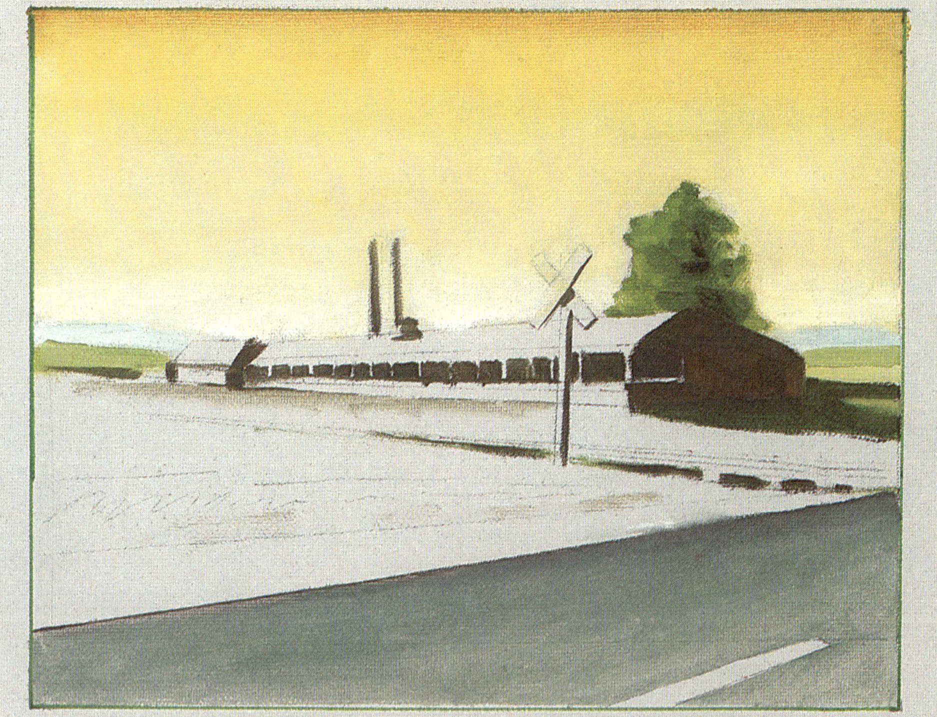

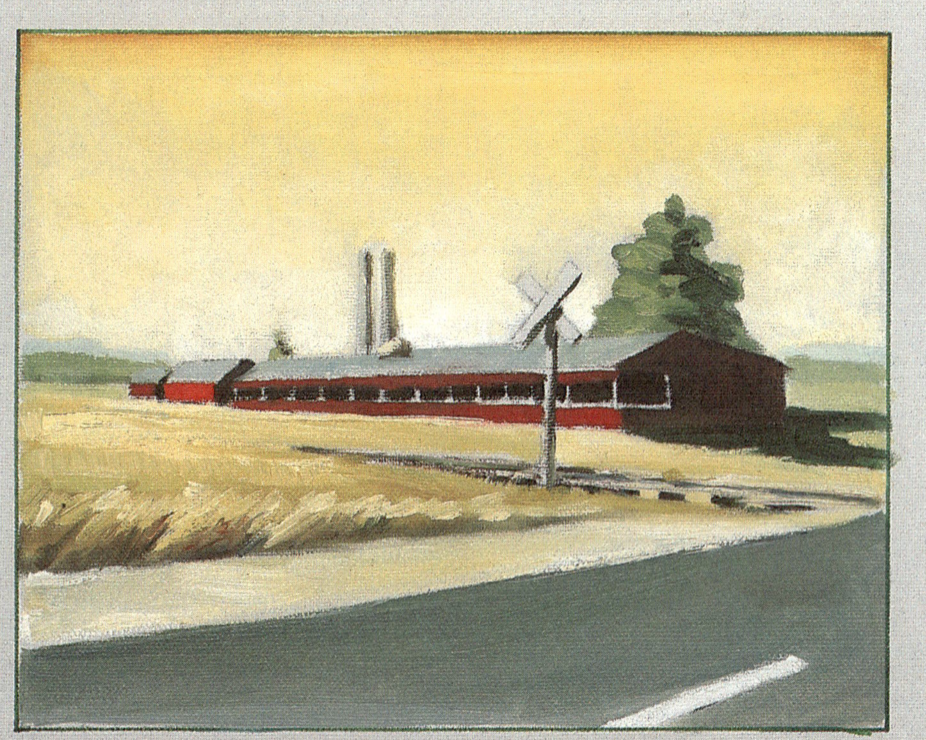

It is very important that you get the perspective correct in your drawing. Draw an imaginary horizon line near the center of your canvas. Now draw a vertical line that represents the nearest corner of the building. With a straight edge or mahlstick, connect the top of the vertical line and the bottom of the vertical line to an imaginary point on the far left side of the horizon line. Now connect the top of the roof line and the railroad tracks so that they converge at the same point. These guidelines will keep all your elements in perspective.

This is a very warm picture. The sky is Orange, graduated down to Yellow, then to a very Whitish-Yellow hue on the horizon. Cerulean Blue and White delineate the distant hills. The tree is painted with Sap Green and White. Rose Madder is used in painting the shadows of the building. The combination of Blue, Green and Orange is the initial color used to paint the highway.

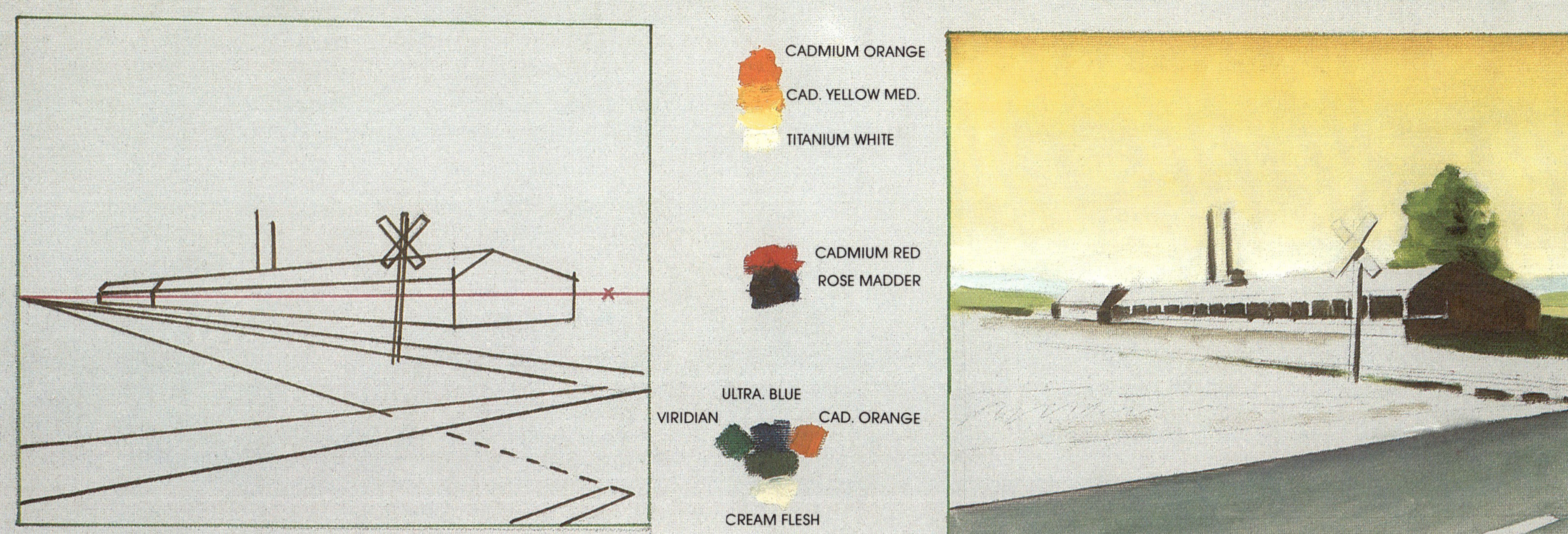

Up until now I have used round and bright sable brushes. The grass and weeds needed thicker paint to depict them properly, so I switched to a filbert brush.

The shadows of the grass are Raw Sienna with some Terra Rosa added. Yellow Ochre is the predominant color, with Naples Yellow for the highlights. Cream Flesh is then used to depict the roadside. The asphalt was a little too Blue, so when it dried I put a wash of Sap Green over it.

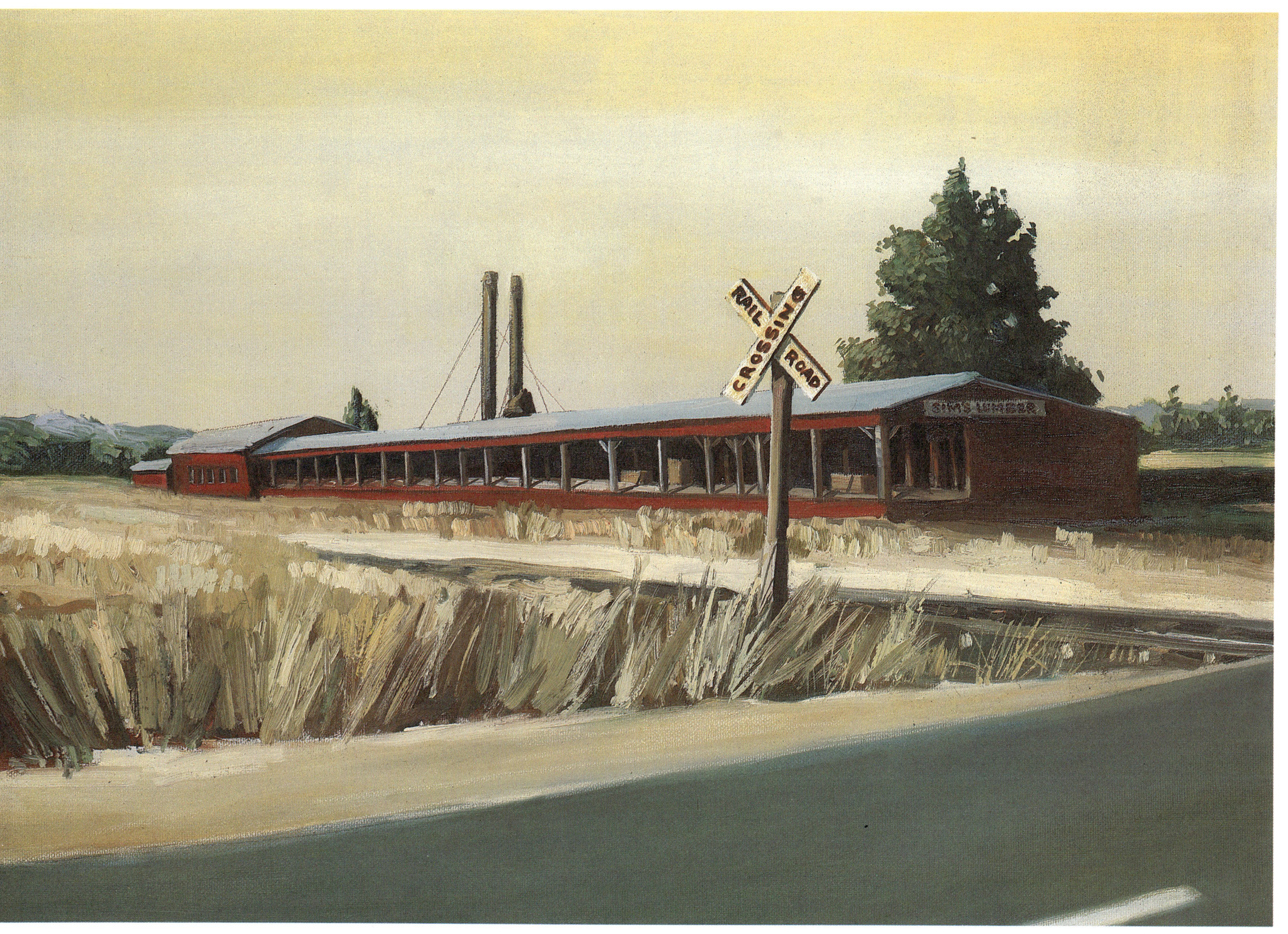

This painting is extremely simple in its design elements. The formula, however, works very well. It seems people never tire of old shacks, barns or run-down buildings. The key element is, of course, the perspective.

Study the vanishing point. You will notice that the parallel lines converge at a point on the horizon, creating an optical illusion.

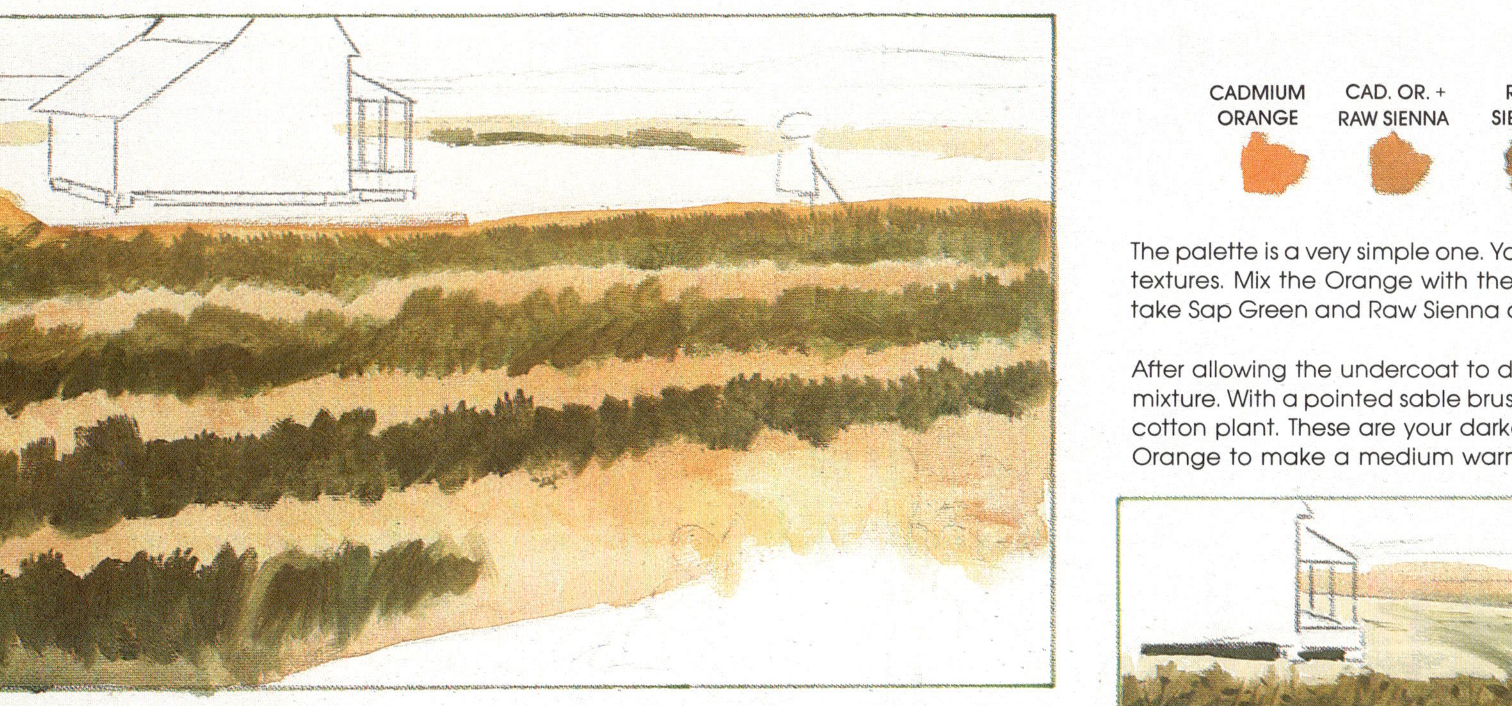

CADMIUM ORANGE — CAD. OR. + RAW SIENNA — RAW SIENNA — RAW SIENNA + SAP GR. — SAP GREEN

The palette is a very simple one. Your only concerns should be the values and textures. Mix the Orange with the Raw Sienna and lay down a wash. Next, take Sap Green and Raw Sienna and "scumble" the cotton rows.

After allowing the undercoat to dry, mix a very dark Green and Raw Sienna mixture. With a pointed sable brush, indicate the leaves and the stems of the cotton plant. These are your darkest values. Next, mix some Sap Green and Orange to make a medium warm Green and repeat the previous process.

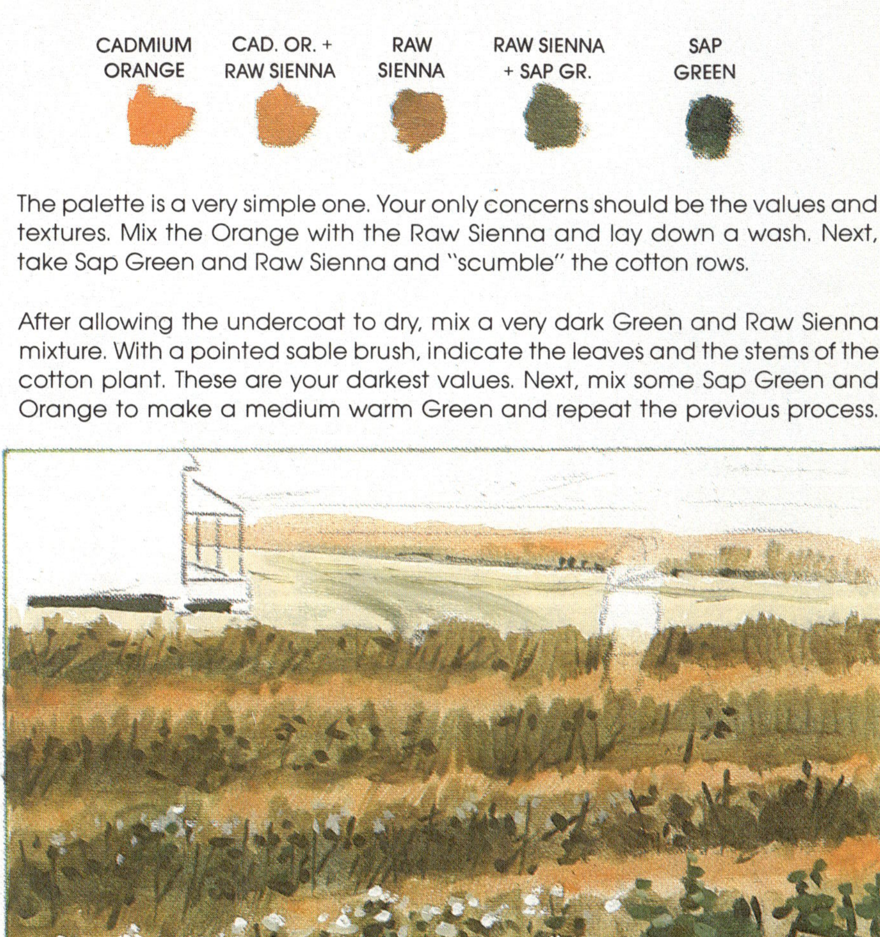

Add a little Cream Flesh to your Green and indicate a few highlights on the plants. The cotton balls are Off White with White highlights. You can daub these on with a round bristle brush. I also painted some green plants in the right hand corner to break up the reddish-brown.

No time is spent on the house or the figure here. These subjects have been covered in previous paintings. The novice will often shy away from a scene like this. As you can see, what seems complicated can be easily rendered when reduced to these simple steps.

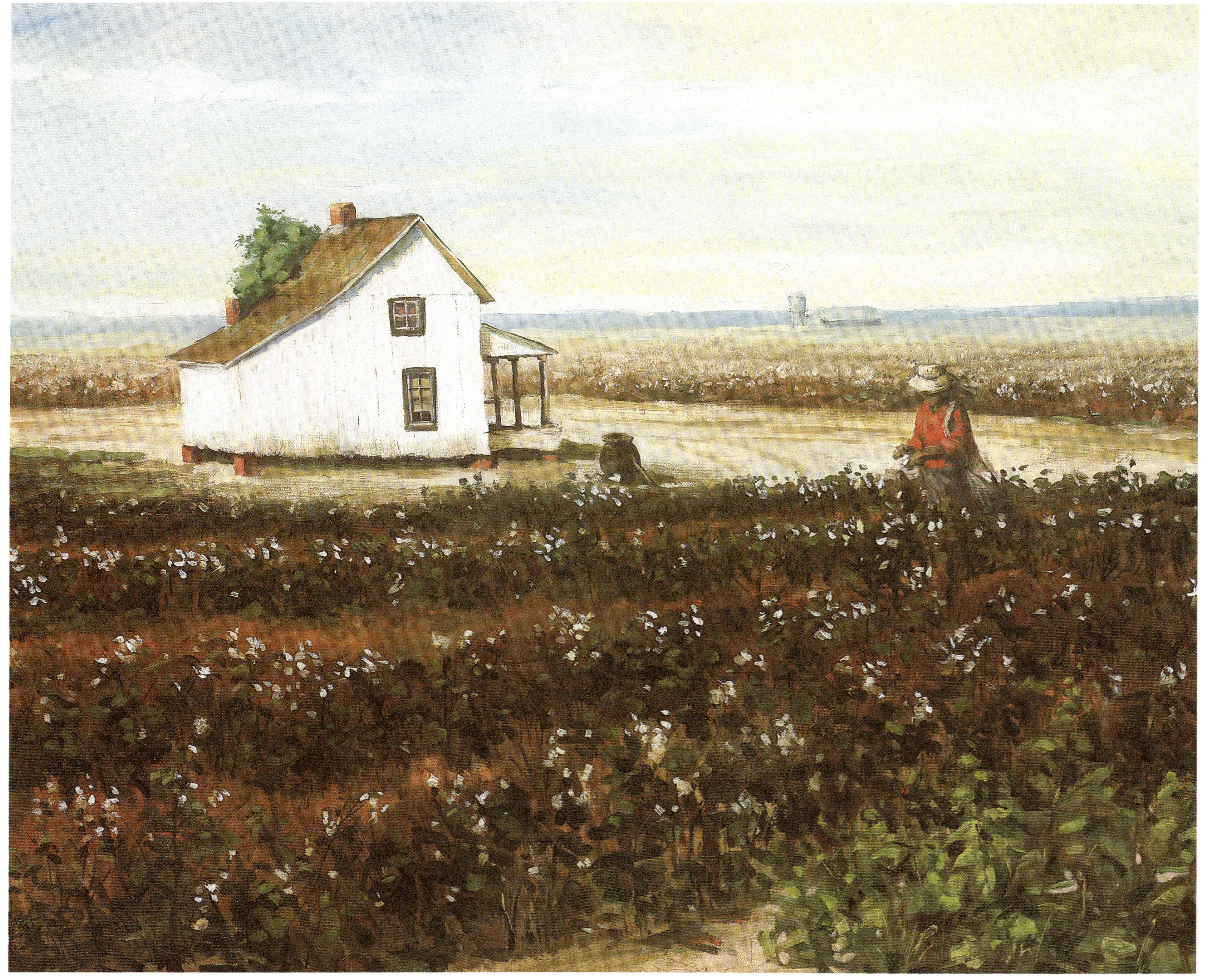

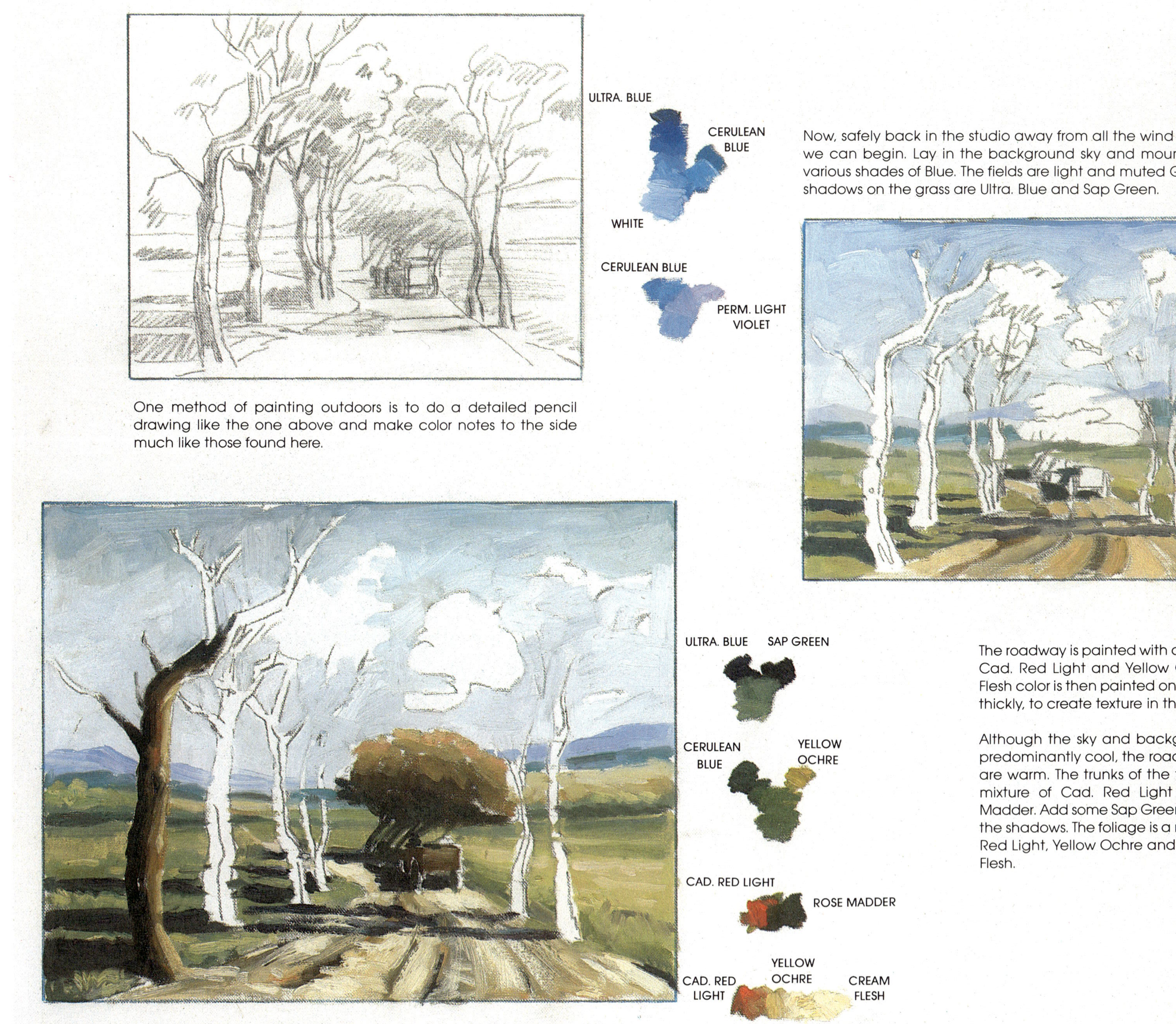

Now, safely back in the studio away from all the wind and bugs, we can begin. Lay in the background sky and mountains with various shades of Blue. The fields are light and muted Greens. The shadows on the grass are Ultra. Blue and Sap Green.

One method of painting outdoors is to do a detailed pencil drawing like the one above and make color notes to the side much like those found here.

The roadway is painted with a mixture of Cad. Red Light and Yellow Ochre. The Flesh color is then painted on top, rather thickly, to create texture in the road.

Although the sky and background are predominantly cool, the road and trees are warm. The trunks of the trees are a mixture of Cad. Red Light and Rose Madder. Add some Sap Green to darken the shadows. The foliage is a mix of Cad. Red Light, Yellow Ochre and Traditional Flesh.

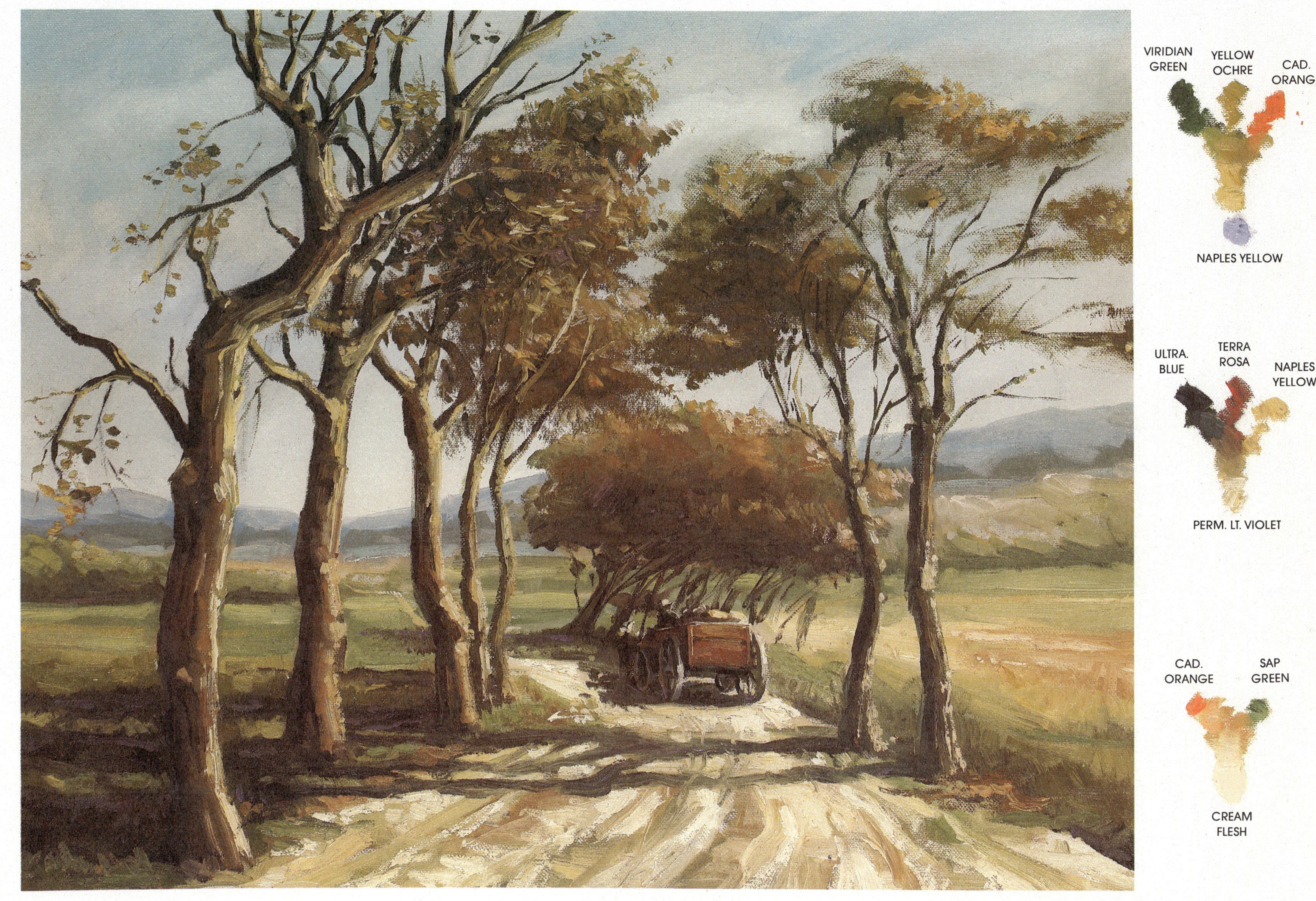

The impressionist painters never seemed to tire of this subject. Neither do I. Roads leading somewhere — to town or to a farmhouse for instance — draw the viewer into the painting. If you study Sisley and Pissaro you will discover the infinite varieties of ways to utilize this design.

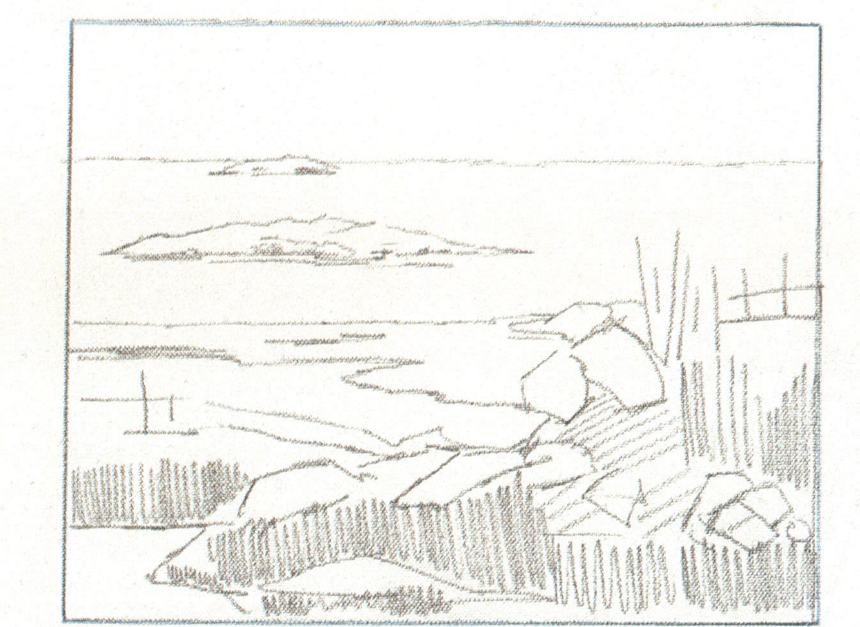

A light pencil sketch is used here to suggest placement of the elements. Here, again, I have reduced the groups of flowers to a very simple shape. Roughly indicate where the dark and light patterns will go.

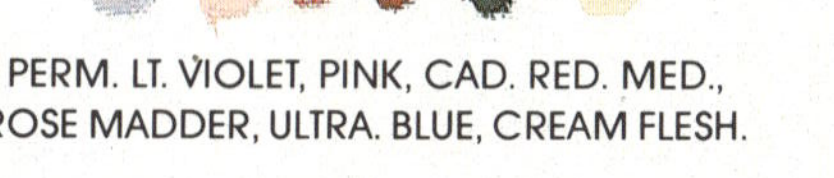

Because it is a simple design, I can block-in all the basic colors very quickly. The sky begins at the top with Cerulean and Cobalt, then gradually becomes lighter at the horizon. The ocean is Bluish-Violet and darker in value. The grassy cliff is dark and light Viridian.

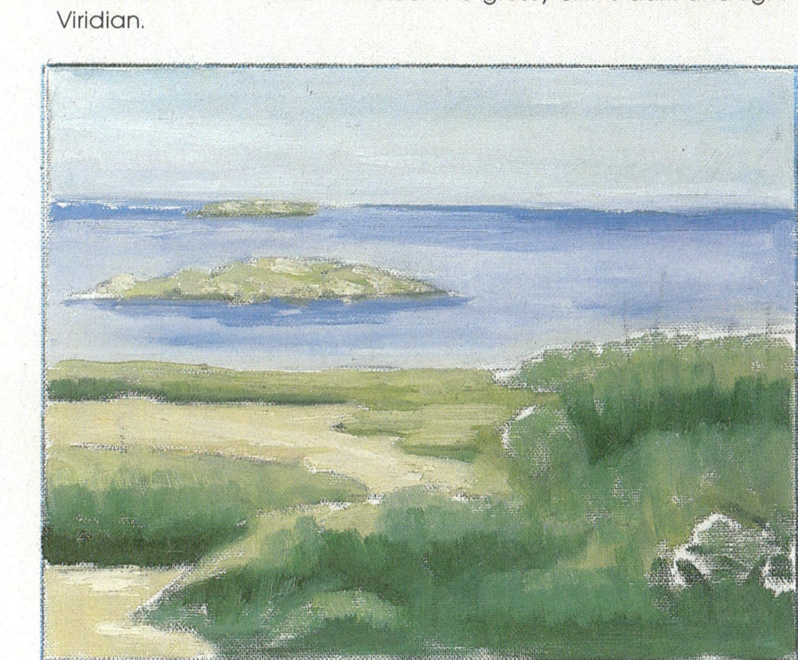

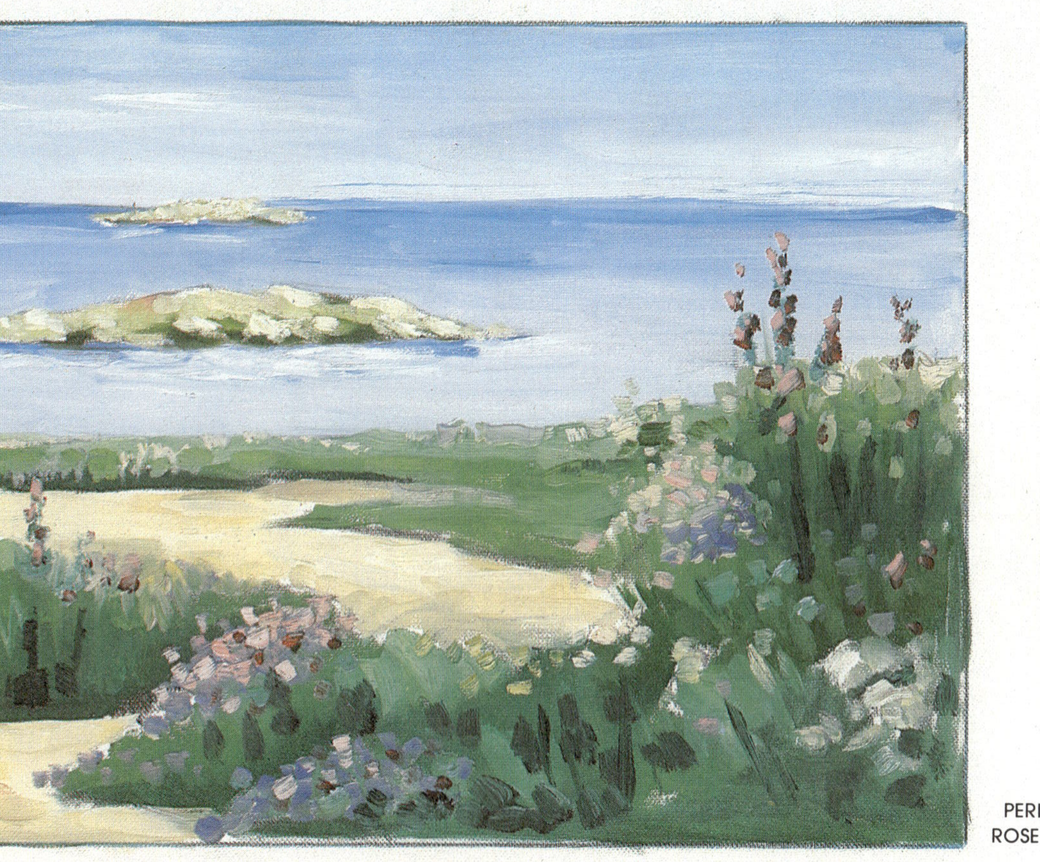

After blocking-in, I look for the darkest darks. With a round sable brush I begin to indicate the lower stems using Ultra. Blue and Viridian. Using a lighter Green, I paint in some leaves using short, choppy strokes. To complete the picture, I take a bristle flat and a pointed palette knife and paint the flowers with light and dark Purples, Pinks and Reds.

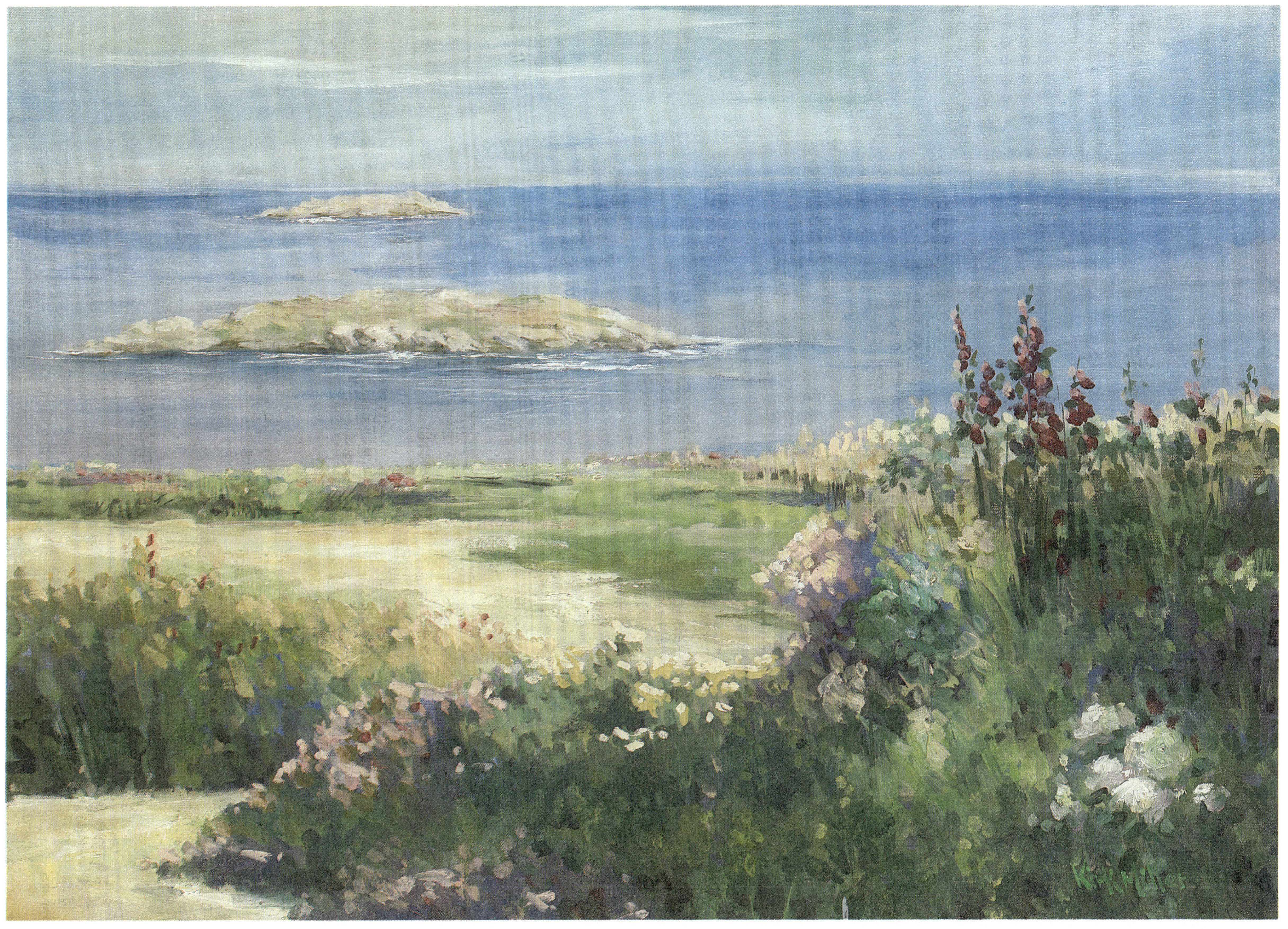

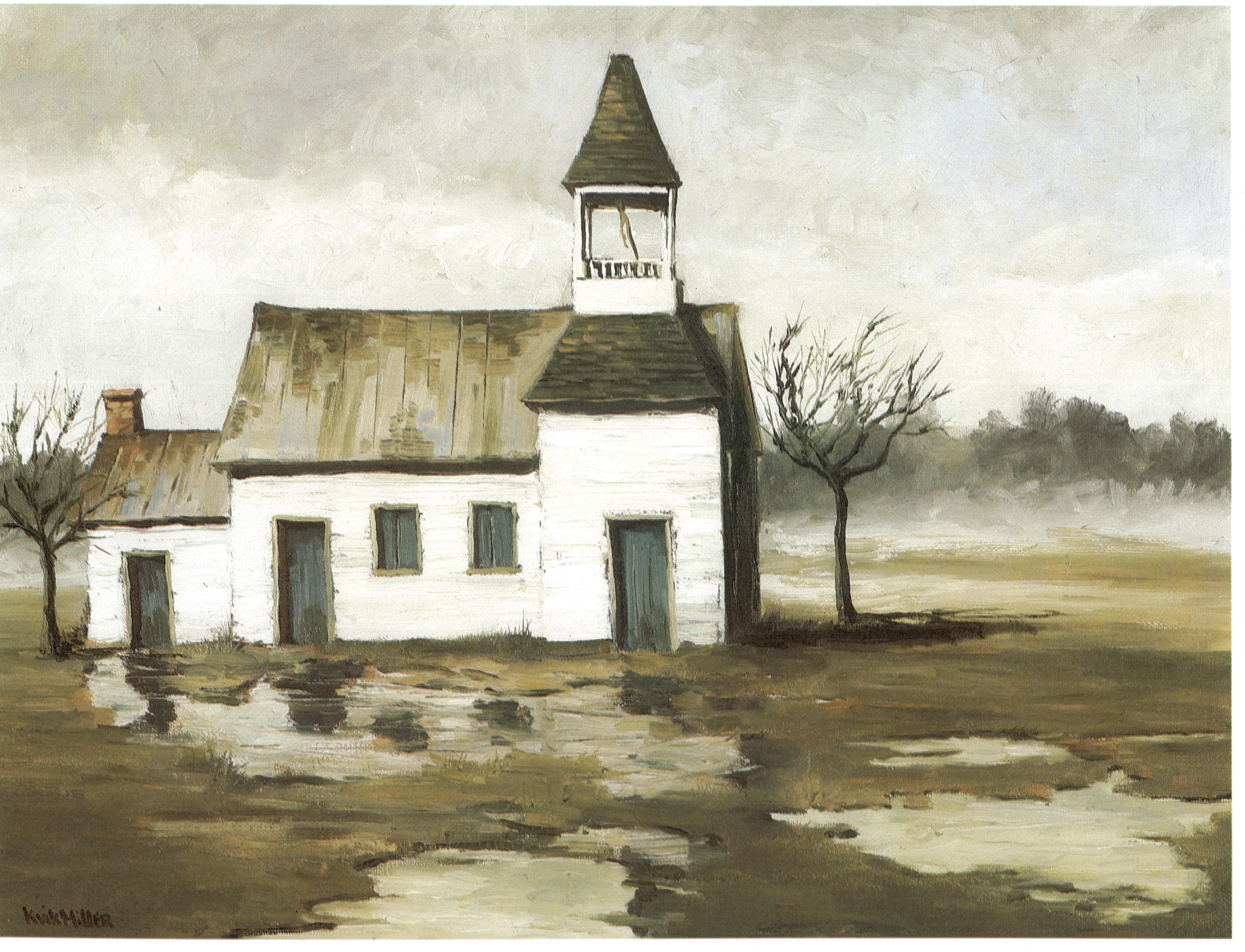

If you desire a more moody or somber effect in a landscape, just select a gloomy scene. Here we have an old weathered church shortly after a rainstorm. The trees are without foliage, the stark white of the church and the cold green shutters and doors combine to create the desired effect.

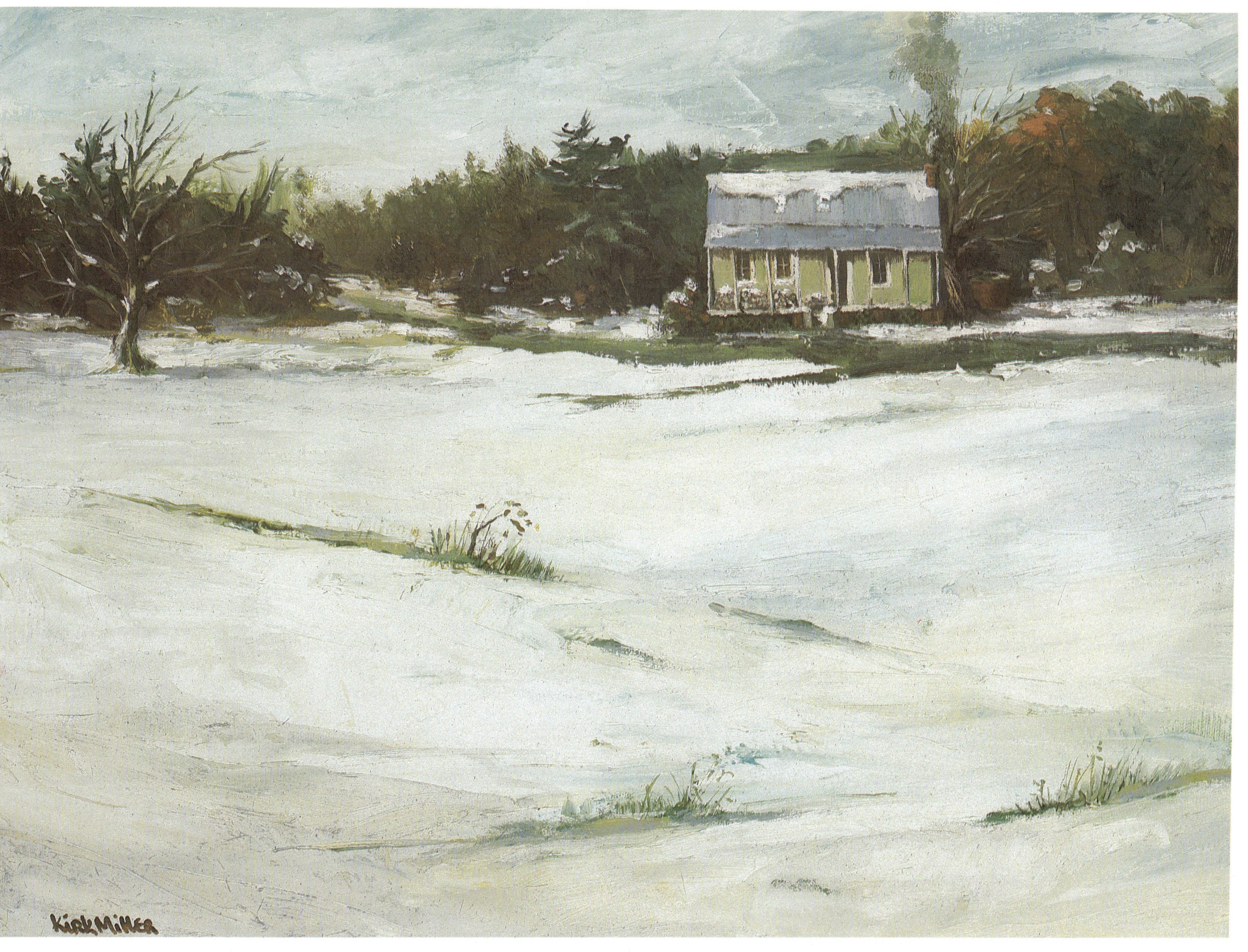

I have not spent a great deal of time in snow country, but enough to get by. I salute the artists who stand knee-deep in the snow and fight with their paints as they freeze. In any case, I have tried to convey the cold and slush with a hint of warmth radiating from the inside of the farmhouse.

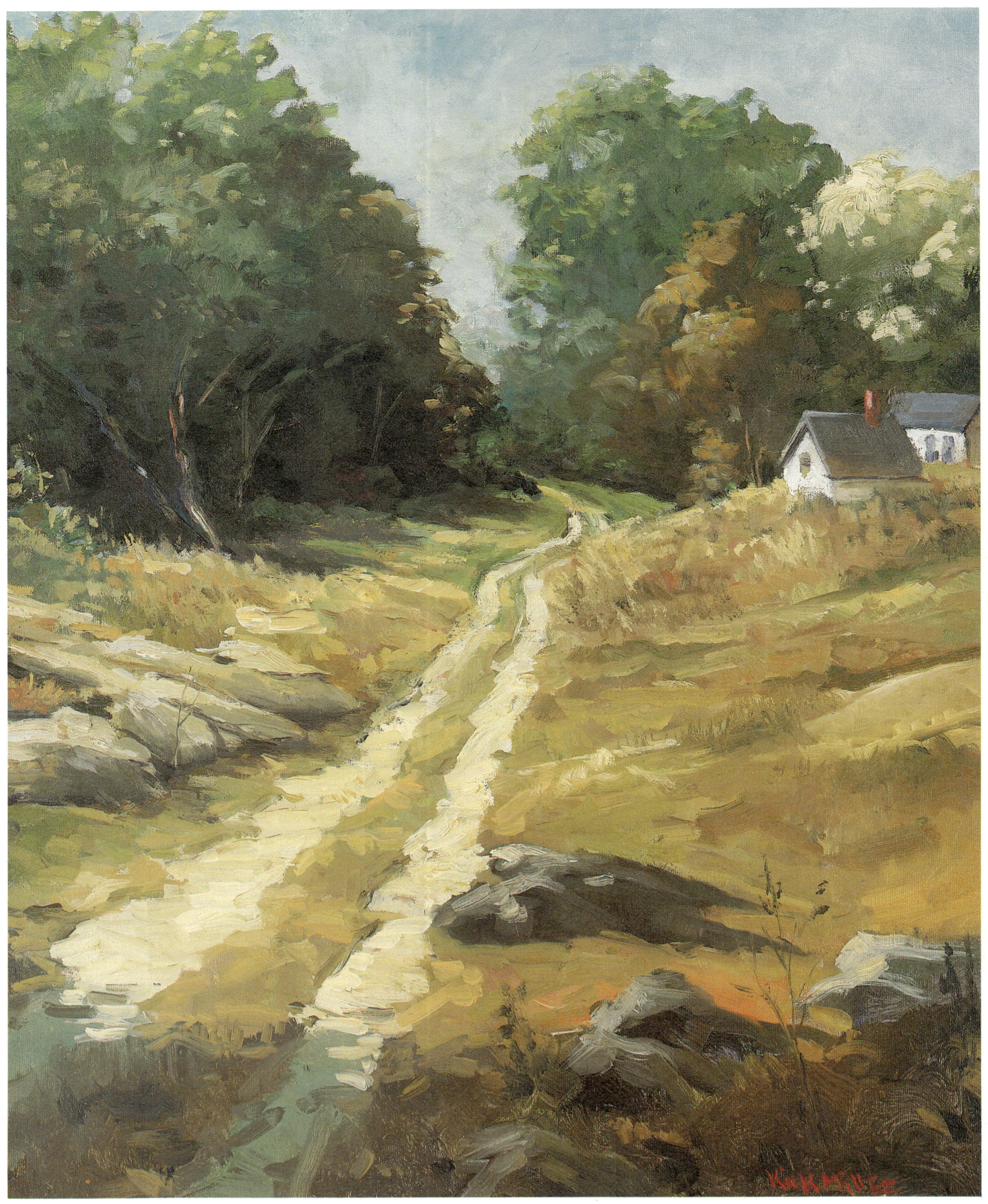

On page 4, I discussed using warm primaries or cool primaries, exclusively, to paint a picture. Here are two examples of that approach.

It takes a long time and a great deal of patience to paint this way. Just mixing all the colors is a task in itself. However, the results can be quite pleasing.

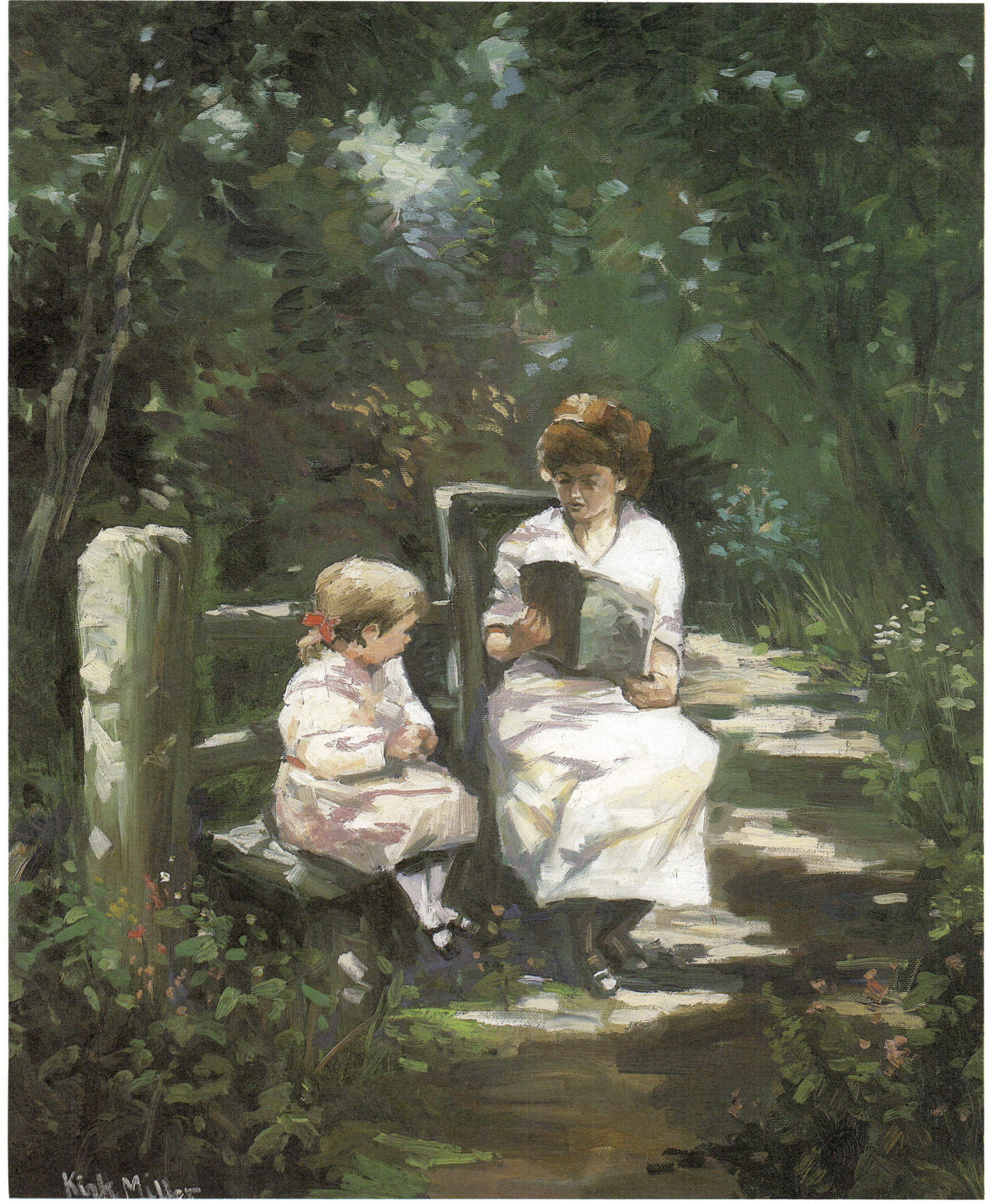

COOL

PARTING OBSERVATIONS

It has been my experience that landscape painting affords the artist with the greatest variety of subjects and the largest audience for potential sales. Regardless of the style one chooses, the variety of subjects in nature is infinite.

Not depicted here are cityscapes, seascapes, boat docks, desert scenes and abstractions. For the beginner, intermediate or those with professional pursuits, the landscape can offer great challenges and excitement.

More Ways To Learn...With Walter Foster!

BEGINNERS ART SERIES
Introductory Art Skills

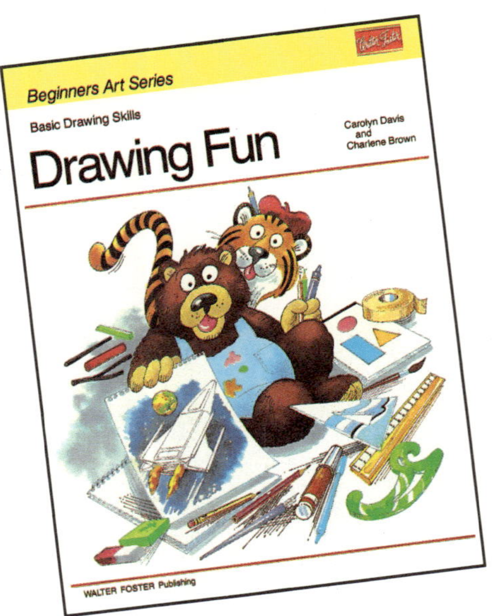

Looking for a way to spend "quality time" with the children in your life? Introduce them to the wonderful world of art...with the **Beginners Art Series** by Walter Foster Publishing. For $5.95 per title, this innovative instructional series teaches them the basics of art and art theory...expands their creativity...and develops their tactile and visual skills. Children ages six and up will be enthralled for hours...whether it's *Drawing Fun, Color*

Fun, Clay Fun, Comic Strip Fun, Poster/ Lettering Fun, Paper Art Fun...or all six titles. Written by experts in art education, these books provide demonstrations with easy-to-understand instructions and follow a standardized format including: a glossary of art vocabulary, a section on materials listing the tools associated with each topic, and a series of exciting projects for "hands on" creative experience.

HOW TO SERIES
Developing Art Skills

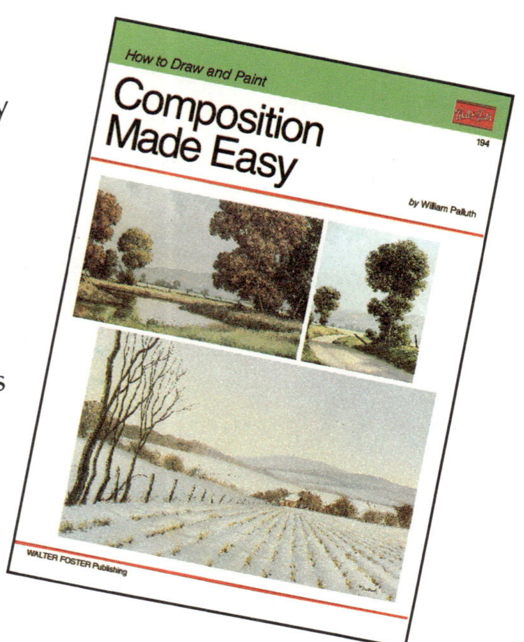

Now you can develop your art skills...easily and economically! The **How To Series** shows you how with art books addressing all media—pencil, watercolor, oil, acrylic, pen & ink, charcoal and pastel...and a variety of subject matter—animals, cartoons, figures, landscapes, seascapes, still life and more.
Written by accomplished artists, the books in the **How To Series** will help you improve your skills to become the best

artist you can be! You will enjoy exploring the basics of form, line and dimension ...and learn the intricacies of advanced rendering techniques. You'll learn secrets that have helped our authors achieve excellence in their artistic specialties. There are over 100 titles in the Walter Foster **How To Series.** At only $3.95 per title these books fit every budget!

ARTIST'S LIBRARY SERIES
Advanced Art Skills

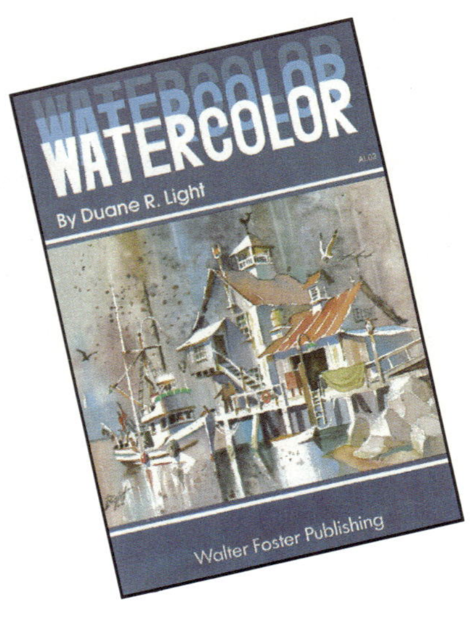

If you're serious about art, you don't want to be without the books in the Walter Foster **Artist's Library Series.** Focusing on a specific medium, subject or technique, each of these books teaches you complete procedures, from beginning to end.
The **Artist's Library Series** offers books addressing oil painting, watercolors, pencil drawing, acrylics, color theory, pen & ink, colored pencils, pastels, airbrush,

calligraphy, impressionism, dry-brush watercolor, perspective and cartooning. You will find that these books are invaluable reference guides...No other texts offer such unique instruction at such a reasonable price—only $5.95 per title. The **Artist's Library Series** is sure to be a welcome addition to your library of art books!

Walter Foster Publishing ... The most recognized name in art publishing for more than 73 years.